Sex in Prison

Sex in Prison

The Mississippi Experiment
with Conjugal Visiting

COLUMBUS B. HOPPER

Louisiana State University Press   Baton Rouge

To men in prisons

Copyright © 1969 by
Louisiana State University Press

Library of Congress Catalog Card Number 70–86491
SBN 8071–0905–3
Manufactured in the United States of America by
The Parthenon Press, Nashville, Tennessee

Designed by Jules B. McKee

Acknowledgments

I would like to express my appreciation to the administrative officers and staff of the Mississippi State Penitentiary for granting me permission to make this study and for their time, help, and courtesy during its course. I would like to thank, especially, Mr. C. E. Breazeale and Mr. Thomas D. Cook, superintendents of the penitentiary during the years when the study was made. This study is due, in large part, to their professional orientation toward corrections and their respect for the research process and its products. Mr. John D. Johnson of Natchez, Mississippi, made the photographs included in the book.

I would also like to acknowledge the help given me by the inmates of the Mississippi State Penitentiary. In no instance was an inmate uncooperative. Many inmates gave much of their free time in interviews, for which I am deeply grateful.

Contents

	Acknowledgments	vii
	Introduction	3
I	The Penitentiary	17
II	The Conjugal Visit	49
III	Why Conjugal Visiting in Mississippi?	64
IV	Evaluations and Attitudes	84
V	Conjugal Visiting and Prisonization	110
VI	A Look to the Future	137
	Bibliography	149
	Index	157

Sex in Prison

Introduction

In recent years American criminologists and penologists have given increased attention to the contacts which inmates of correctional institutions have with persons from outside the institution. There is a general recognition that the inmate must be considered not only as an individual but as an individual who is a member of an outside group or groups in which his ultimate adjustment must be effected. Competent correctional administrators have noted, and research has confirmed, that prisoners who have constructive relationships with people from the outside are more likely to do well in prison and later on parole than those who do not.[1] A 1954 report by the Committee on Classification and Casework of the American Prison Association indicated that all inmates need to retain, or develop anew, such relationships and that no matter what the staff of a prison may do on behalf of the inmate, as long as he has no genuine contacts with the "real world," the obstacles to his adjustment and rehabilitation are great.

[1] See Norman Fenton (ed.), *Handbook on the Inmate's Relationships with Persons Outside the Adult Correctional Institution* (American Prison Association, Committee on Classification and Casework, 1953).

The type of contact which married male prisoners are allowed to maintain with their wives has long been of interest to those involved in correctional research.[2] Although there is agreement that the inmate's wife should be allowed to visit her husband within the prison, American prison officials generally have not given married prisoners many privileges in this regard. Almost all American penal institutions permit spouses to visit within the prison, but almost without exception these visits are brief and infrequent. Visits of not over two hours twice a month form the most typical pattern, and even then husbands and wives visit in a room usually crowded with other inmates and visitors.[3] More often than not, these visits are under the close scrutiny of prison guards. In some instances an inmate and his wife must visit with a glass or wire partition between them, or by telephone. From the standpoint of American prison practice, permission to have a wife or other relative visit an inmate is a very special privilege and not a right.

There is, however, one important exception to the American visitation privileges described above. At the Mississippi State Penitentiary a system of conjugal visitation has developed in which the institution allows wives of prisoners to visit their husbands and provides facilities for them to spend time together in private. When a prisoner's wife comes to visit him, he is permitted to go with her to

[2] Eugene S. Zemans and Ruth S. Cavan, "Marital Relationships of Prisoners," *Journal of Criminal Law, Criminology and Police Science*, LXVIII (1958), 50–57. See also Norman Fenton, *The Prisoner's Family* (Palo Alto, 1959).

[3] Zemans and Cavan, "Marital Relationships of Prisoners," 52.

a building divided into private rooms. In this building, the couple may have sexual relations. Although the California Correctional Institute at Tehachapi in 1968 began an experimental program by allowing a few inmates nearing the end of their sentences to spend a weekend with their wives in apartments on the prison grounds, the Mississippi State Penitentiary is the only penal institution in the United States which permits conjugal visits for all married men throughout their prison sentences.[4] At least, it is the only prison which has publicly announced that it does.

The type of contact which the married male prisoner is allowed to have with his wife varies in countries other than the United States, and descriptions of the privileges that exist are not detailed. The most comprehensive survey to date was made in 1963 by Luzian Verborgen, a German writer and criminologist at the University of Hamburg.[5] Although it is difficult to generalize about the privileges allowed due to variations within individual countries, one learns from Verborgen's report that in most nations the possibility of conjugal visits during the course of a prison sentence does not exist. While information about many countries could not be obtained, it was definitely established that in thirty-nine countries neither conjugal visits nor home furloughs are allowed. These are: Afghanistan, Australia, Austria, British Gambia, Cambodia, Cyprus,

---

[4] *Time,* August 9, 1968, p. 68.

[5] Von Luzian Verborgen, "Freiheitsstrafvollug und Ehelicher Umgang," *Monatsschrift Fur Kriminologie Und Strafrechtareform,* XLVIII (1958), 410–13.

the Dominican Republic, Ethiopia, Finland, France, Ghana, Haiti, Hungary, Iceland, Indonesia, Iran, Iraq, the Islam Republic, Italy, Liberia, Luxemburg, Mauretania, Morocco, The Netherlands, Nicaragua, the Nigerian Federation, Norway, Panama, Paraguay, Portugal, Portuguese Guinea, Senegal, the Union of South Africa, Spain, Switzerland, Thailand, Turkey, Uruguay, and the United Arab Republic.

In other nations, married inmate privileges include conjugal visits or furloughs, and in some places both furloughs and conjugal visiting. Countries allowing furloughs only are: Argentina, Belgium, Czechoslovakia, Denmark, West Germany, Great Britain, Greece, Ireland, and the Sudan. Those in which only conjugal visits are allowed are: Burma, Chile, Costa Rica, Equador, El Salvador, Guatemala, Honduras, Japan, Mexico, Peru, the Philippine Islands, and the Soviet Union. Countries where both conjugal visits and home furloughs were granted were: Bolivia, Brazil, Canada, Colombia, India, Pakistan, Poland, Puerto Rico, Sweden, and Venezuela.

In the Soviet Union men in prison are allowed conjugal visits from their wives once a month. Wives are brought to the prison at government expense and stay in a special building with their husbands for several days. Soviet prison authorities praise conjugal visits and believe that the practice keeps the rate of homosexuality low in their prisons.[6]

Male prisoners in Mexico have traditionally had conjugal visiting privileges, usually once a week in their cells.

[6] Peter Landermann, "Life as a Soviet Prisoner," *Saturday Evening Post,* January 15, 1966, p. 32.

Until about 1950, this privilege could be enjoyed by all male prisoners whether they were married or not. Currently, however, most Mexican prisons allow conjugal visits only for inmates who have wives, common-law wives, or properly recognized consorts. In some instances, prison officials have allowed a single prisoner to marry and spend a honeymoon of two or three days in his cell.[7]

Mexican officials strongly feel that conjugal visits help prevent homosexuality. Furthermore, they believe the practice helps preserve the nation's strong family tradition. Mexican prisoners consider the conjugal visit a "right" rather than a privilege. In 1947, for example, the program was abolished in the Federal Penitentiary in Mexico City, but it was restored after a week of rioting by the prisoners.[8]

Sweden is an interesting example of the countries in which conjugal association is possible through prison visits as well as home furloughs. In the minimum security institutions in Sweden, conjugal visits are permitted in the prisoners' cells. In institutions housing inmates who must be guarded very closely, conjugal visits are not allowed as freely, but they may occur. On the average in Sweden's institutions, conjugal visits are allowed once a month. Furloughs are also very important in Sweden's penal system, and are extended to single inmates as well as to married men. Before a furlough is granted, a prisoner is expected to have served approximately one-third of his sentence; in the case of life imprisonment, at least three years must have been served. The frequency of furloughs

[7] "Wedlock in the Cellblock," *Time*, May 5, 1952, p. 25.
[8] "Black Palace," *Life*, April 3, 1950, p. 113.

in some prisons is every three months and in others every four months. The first furlough an inmate receives does not exceed forty-eight hours, and succeeding furloughs are limited to seventy-two hours.

The variations and lack of specificity in conjugal privileges in Swedish prisons are typical of those in most countries. The rules governing conjugal visits and furloughs rest in part on official rules, in part on unwritten agreements among the prison directors, and are usually administered by the authorities at their own discretion. Despite the report that about 15 percent of the inmates in Sweden violate their furloughs, prison authorities say they are satisfied with the success of the program.

Sweden has also begun allowing some prisoners to serve the last portion of their sentences in the free community.[9] Unlike parolees, the live-out prisoners have their rent subsidized by the state, the goal being to ease the transition to civilian life for convicts with good records. The only requirement for the prisoners living outside the institution is that they must check in regularly with a prison official. This program is available for unmarried as well as married prisoners.

Denmark is representative of countries allowing furloughs but not conjugal visits within prisons. In that country, furloughs of several days (usually five to seven) are permitted in some prisons after six months of a prisoner's term has been served. In other prisons, however, an inmate must have served at least one year. The frequency of leaves

[9] *Time,* September 22, 1967, p. 38.

also varies. In Great Britain, prisoners who are serving sentences of two or more years may have furloughs of five days near the end of their imprisonment. In Ireland, also, furloughs are granted every weekend during the final six months of imprisonment, but not at earlier stages of sentences.

Six countries permit some inmates to live with their wives in penal colonies. These are: Burma, India, Mexico, Pakistan, the Philippines, and the Soviet Union. In the Philippines much emphasis is placed upon family living for prisoners. Each family in a penal colony is supported by the state at first, but eventually most families can provide for their livelihood out of the profits from their own work. The state assumes the family's travel expenses to the colony. Marriages also are allowed for single inmates, and fiancées are permitted to travel to the colonies for their weddings at the state's expense. Family prisons have been in existence in the Philippines for over fifty years and appear to be firmly established in prison philosophy and practice there.

In India, selected prisoners are allowed to live with their families in a colony near Bombay. Usually these are prisoners sentenced for life who have earned their way to the colony by good behavior in other prisons. The couples live in separate cottages and wear civilian clothes. Most of them have jobs which allow them to sustain their families with little expense to the state.

Mexico has instituted a family prison worthy of note. This interesting institution, the Tres Marias Penal Colony, is located about ninety miles off the Pacific coast near

San Blas. Maria Madre, one of four islands purchased from private owners by the Mexican government in 1905, was at first used virtually as a slave labor camp for Mexico's worst offenders. As described in recent years, however, the island has evolved into one of the world's most liberal correctional institutions.[10]

The Tres Marias Penal Colony usually has about eight-hundred prisoners who come from other federal penitentiaries throughout Mexico. Interestingly enough, prison colonists are selected from among those who have long records of previous offenses, or who were convicted of murder, assaults, or other serious crimes. They nearly always have twenty or more years to serve. Women prisoners are also accepted at the prison; normally, about twenty women are confined on the island. Upon his arrival at the colony, a prisoner is temporarily assigned to a barracks where he lives until he has served six months with good behavior. Then he is allowed to select a site for his home in anticipation of his family's arrival.

A prisoner has complete freedom of the island's thirty-four thousand acres. He is free to pursue an occupation of his choice, the only requirement being that he observe regular working hours. He may farm or establish himself in a trade or business, tax free. There are also industrial plants on the island owned by private companies which may employ him. Thirty percent of his wages are set aside and returned to him upon his parole or discharge. The

[10] Donald P. Jewell, "Mexico's Tres Marias Penal Colony," *Journal of Criminal Law, Criminology and Police Science*, XLVIII (1958), 410–13.

island is, in fact, a community with schools, churches, and other social organizations; here a prisoner can live with his wife and children very much like he would in any other community. He does not wear a prison uniform except one day a month when he has to appear before a counseling board. Both male and female single inmates are allowed to marry and bring their spouses to the colony.

In some Latin American countries, not only married men but single prisoners as well may have sex relations with women from outside the prison while serving sentences. In Colombia, inmates may leave prison once every two weeks, under guard, to visit a licensed house of prostitution. The length of these visits is two hours.

It seems impossible to detect any meaningful pattern in countries which permit conjugal visits as compared to those which do not. The practice is found in many places under greatly different societal conditions. One is able to say, however, that it has become more widespread in recent years even though it is still not accepted by a majority of countries. It is now extensive enough to be considered well on its way to becoming a significant if not an integral part of modern penology. Canada adopted conjugal visiting in 1960. A new prison law passed in that year specifically made provisions for conjugal visits as well as for home furloughs. The Canadian authorities recommended conjugal visits on humanitarian grounds as well as for rehabilitation of inmates. In conjunction with furloughs, conjugal visits have been credited with saving family relationships, relieving tensions, and introducing a higher level of morality within prisons.[11]

Canada's Saskatchewan Correctional Centre in Regina in April of 1968 instituted a family counseling program which includes conjugal visits. Prisoners are allowed to have visits from their wives twice a week in a newly built duplex equipped with two-bedroom suites. Although the duplex is outside the institutional fence, it is located on the institutional grounds near a staff residential area. Except for counseling sessions, families are unsupervised while at the prison. Lengths of visits vary from an afternoon to two days and nights. The number of inmates involved in the program at any one time is usually around fifteen. The program has been well received by the staff members as well as inmates.[12]

Conjugal visiting has been proposed from time to time as a partial solution to sexual problems in prisons in the United States. Recently, for example, conjugal visiting was one of several recommendations made in a report dealing with a series of homosexual rapes of young men in Philadelphia prisons.[13] Former warden of San Quentin Clinton Duffy has strongly advocated the use of conjugal visits to relieve what he called "massive sexual frustration" in

[11] Verborgen, "Freiheitsstrafvollug und Ehelicher Umgang," 413.

[12] Personal correspondence from Mr. D. G. Macknak, family therapist, Saskatchewan Correctional Centre, Canada, February, 1969.

[13] *Report on Sexual Assaults in the Philadelphia Prison System and Sheriff's Vans* (Philadelphia, 1968). This report was the result of an investigation ordered by Judge Alexander F. Barbieri of the Court of Common Pleas. The investigation was conducted by Alan Davies, Special Master of Prison Abuses in Philadelphia County.

American prisons.[14] Those in charge of our prisons have
generally concluded, however, that conjugal visits would
be wholly unrealistic in the American culture and that
they would tend to heighten rather than relieve tension in
our prisons.[15] As a consequence of this reasoning, prison
officials in the United States have believed they were
powerless to do anything about the sexual problems in
prison. A survey of American prison wardens in 1964
showed that only 13.4 percent were in favor of conjugal
visits, and that most were very definitely opposed to
them.[16] Most penal administrators in this country apparently agree with the secretary of the American Correctional Association who, in speaking of conjugal visiting,
recently said: "This system is nothing more than a legal
house of prostitution." [17]

The chief objection to conjugal visits in the United
States is the belief that they would be incompatible with
existing mores, since the visits seem to emphasize only the
physical satisfactions of sex. Another objection is based
upon the conviction that married inmates who could
satisfactorily engage in conjugal visits are those who can
adjust best to prison life even without sex relations; likewise, those inmates who present the greatest sexual prob-

[14] Clinton T. Duffy, "Prison Problem Nobody Talks About,"
This Week Magazine, October 21, 1962, pp. 13–14.
[15] Paul W. Tappan, *Crime, Justice and Correction* (New York,
1960) , 680.
[16] Joseph K Balough, "Conjugal Visitations in Prisons: A Sociological Perspective," *Federal Probation,* XXVIII (1964) , 52–58.
[17] Dr. E. Preston Sharp of Washington, D.C., is quoted in Baton
Rouge *State-Times,* January 5, 1968. He was interviewed following
a tour of the Louisiana State Prison Farm at Angola.

lems, i.e., homosexuals and other sex deviates, are the ones
least likely to benefit from conjugal visits.

Additional objections are that conjugal visits offer no
solution to the sexual tensions of either single male prisoners or female prisoners, and that the prisoners' wives
may become pregnant, creating further problems for both
the state and the prisoners, especially for long-term inmates.[18] Others reject the practice because of financial limitations, fear of unfavorable public reaction, custody and
security problems, or the belief that it will lead to prison
corruption as well as lessen human dignity. Some administrators still feel that the privilege is too lenient and that it
takes away part of the deprivation which they contend is
the chief purpose of imprisonment. In their opinion,
prisons should be "tough" institutions in which punishment prevails with little thought or concern given to
privileges of any sort.

In view of such objections to the conjugal visit, one
would expect that it would be almost impossible for the
practice to develop in the United States. Nevertheless,
conjugal visiting has become an important part of the
Mississippi State Penitentiary system. It has been integrated into a program in which not only wives but also
children are allowed to visit; it has been in existence for a
number of years and gives the appearance of being a permanent adaptation. Although most criminologists and
penologists in the United States have become aware of the

---

[18] Conjugal visits have never been recommended for female prisoners in America.

program, it has received remarkably little attention.[19] It is the purpose of this book, therefore, to present the findings of my study of the program as it is practiced in Mississippi so that students of penal institutions will be able to better evaluate its relevance for use in other prisons in America. I believe conjugal visiting deserves serious consideration by those who seek to allow more normal sexual adjustment among the inmates of American penal institutions.

The research upon which this book is based has utilized questionnaires, personal interviews, and observation. The questionnaire data were collected in October and November of 1963. The descriptive and practical data, however, have been gathered by interviews and observation at various times throughout the course of ten years. On many occasions, the writer has spent an entire day, and often well into the night, in the penitentiary.

The intimate nature of conjugal visiting has posed something of a problem in research methodology. In all cases the privacy of prisoners and their wives has been considered. A minimum of time has been spent in talking to couples on visiting days, in part because on visiting days all visitors, whether wives, parents, or other family members, are more emotional and more easily antagonized or

[19] Most knowledge of the practice has been limited to personal communication at meetings and a brief article or two in popular magazines. See Ernest A. Mitler, "Family Visits Inside a Prison," *Parade*, May 17, 1959, pp. 8–11. The first, and most significant, professional notice came at the Fourth Conference on Corrections held at Florida State University in 1959. The superintendent of the Mississippi State Penitentiary at that time, Mr. William Harpole, appeared on the program and described the practice.

upset than at other times. This is understandable when one realizes that a prisoner and his visitors have only a short time with each other and would not like to spend that time talking with a researcher. In cases where visitors are not able to come to the penitentiary very often, this is doubly true. Consequently, interviews have purposely been conducted on other days, even though in the case of wives this has meant fewer interviews and the necessity of visiting them in their homes.

Chapter I

The Penitentiary

The Mississippi State Penitentiary encompasses twenty-one thousand acres of rich plantation land. The central plantation and the offices of administration are located at Parchman in Sunflower County in the Yazoo-Mississippi Delta about 130 miles northwest of Jackson, the state capital. Parchman, as the institution is popularly called, is one of the world's largest penal farm or plantation systems. It is the only prison for adult felons in the state. To understand the present penal system in Mississippi, however, one must know something of its background and development, for the penal plantation is an adaptation which came about only after other experiments had failed. It is the only system that has proved to be stable in the history of Mississippi penology.

The first state prison in Mississippi was opened on April 15, 1840, in Jackson on the grounds now occupied by the state capitol, with twenty-eight white prisoners on the roll.[1] Prior to that time, the detention of convicts had been the responsibility of each county. Some of the more thickly settled counties having strong jails had for some time been receiving convicts from counties in which fewer people lived. The first centralized state prison was operated in conformity to the Auburn system begun in New

[1] Paul B. Foreman and Julien R. Tatum, "A Short History of Mississippi's Penal System," *Mississippi Law Journal,* X (1938), 256.

York in 1819 in which inmates were kept in solitary confinement at night but worked in association with other prisoners during the day. The Jackson prison contained 150 cells furnished only with a Bible and a mattress and covering.

During the years 1840 to 1847, only 220 convicts were sent to the prison at Jackson which was also known as "East Prison" or "The Walls"; by 1852, however, it was overcrowded. Thus, in 1858, the legislature appropriated five thousand dollars to add another tier of cell blocks to the prison. Inmates worked in the making of brick, at mechanical trades, and in the manufacturing of coarse cotton fabrics and bale rope. At times a small profit for the state was realized from the convicts' labors. As early as 1841 a joint committee of the legislature was appointed to investigate charges of cruelty growing out of the death of a convict. As a result, whipping under any circumstances was abolished, and solitary confinement in dark cells on a diet of bread and water was substituted. At the end of a fiscal year on November 27, 1843, the institution recorded a profit of $2,900, a little over a hundred dollars of which had been earned by detaining runaway slaves.[2]

The Civil War brought disorganization to the Mississippi prison system as it did to all phases of life in the state. Authorities attempted for a while to continue the prison's operation, but finally abandoned it. Twenty-five of the worst prisoners were transported to the Alabama prison in the spring of 1863, and forty others were pardoned by the

[2] *Ibid.*, 258.

governor and mustered into the army of the Confederacy. Among the remaining convicts some, particularly older men, were turned out without being pardoned and the rest were distributed among county jails with the state paying for their detention. The prison in Jackson then became a munitions factory for the Confederacy and was operated profitably until it was destroyed by General Sherman's men on May 17, 1863.[3]

Following the war Mississippi, like several other southern states, turned to the practice of leasing its convicts to private companies. However, this early proved to be an unsatisfactory penal practice. Various investigations were held between 1885 and 1888; almost all of them found evidence of brutality and some misuse of funds.[4] As a result of the abuse in the leasing of convicts, the prison system became the dominant issue in elections and legislative proceedings during this period. Consequently, the new state constitution adopted in 1890 provided that after the last day of 1894 the leasing of convicts would be unlawful.[5] The same constitutional convention laid the framework for a penal plantation system by authorizing the succeeding legislature to select land for a penitentiary farm on which convicts could be detained and worked under the direct supervision of penal authorities responsible to a board of control.

In 1894, acting on the 1890 authorization, the legislature

---

[3] *Ibid.*, 259.

[4] For further discussion of the lease system in the South and elsewhere, see Blake McKelvey, *American Prisons* (Chicago, 1936.)

[5] *Mississippi State Constitution,* Art. X, 223–25.

appropriated the money to buy 7,900 acres. Three farms were purchased; one was in Rankin County, another in Hinds County, and the other in Holmes County. These farms were first cultivated in 1895 and in spite of a bad agricultural year, the net profit of the three totaled sixty thousand dollars, a fact which gave the penal plantation system favor with the legislature.[6] Subsequently, in 1900, appropriations were made for the purchase of the large Parchman plantation in Sunflower County, and the convicts were sent to this site. The plantation has had many acres added to it through the years. The original purchase now forms only the heart of the twenty-one thousand acres which comprise the Mississippi State Penitentiary.

During the first half of the twentieth century, Parchman had only the dual purposes of punishment and profit. Along with other southern penal farms—notably those in Arkansas and Louisiana—Parchman established a national image as a prison rife with exploitation, brutality, and degradation. Continuing to the present, the superintendency and other jobs at the prison have largely been patronage posts, and most administrations have rewarded followers by doling out jobs at Parchman. In several gubernatorial campaigns, irregularities at the penitentiary have been among the major issues. Most of the criticism, however, has been concerned with business aspects rather than with brutality to prisoners or with the need for rehabilitation.

Early in 1913, an investigation by Governor Earl Brewer

[6] Foreman and Tatum, "A Short History of Mississippi's Penal System," 261.

uncovered a graft ring at the penitentiary that in its magnitude shocked the entire state. Brewer brought suit against the secretary of the penitentiary for embezzlement after the governor found that proceeds from penitentiary crop sales had not been returned to the general fund. His investigation revealed that some of the penitentiary sergeants had sold both equipment and products and retained the proceeds. Governor Brewer estimated that over $50,000 worth of cottonseed alone had disappeared in 1910 and 1911. The fact that existing records were so inconsistent caused the governor to state:

> It would have been impossible to ascertain the number of cars or tons of seed made on the property, except by resort to the records of carriers, such as the railroads, who kept their own records in detail for their own use. The system of bookkeeping rendered it absolutely impossible to tell what became of the vast amount of supplies purchased by the board of trustees and hauled away by other people. This lives only in the memory of the convicts and others who saw them hauling it away without any idea of the quantity they got.[7]

This investigation set the tone of future penal investigations in Mississippi. Most have called only for closer regulation in the matters of monetary records and bookkeeping.

Unlike many prisons, idleness among prisoners has never been a problem at Parchman. Rather, they have worked from daylight until dark in the woods and fields

[7] *Mississippi House Journal* (1914), 67-68.

of the plantation, frequently under threat of floggings and a variety of "unofficial" techniques such as beatings with chains and blackjacks, and even shooting. Work has been the most important activity in the penitentiary and everything else overshadowed by it. Even medical attention at times has been unavailable to men at work in isolated areas of the plantation. A young man who was an employee at the penitentiary in 1934–35 described the situation then as follows:

> Immediate medical aid is often impossible to obtain due to the exigencies of prison labor. Since hundreds of prisoners are recruited to the fields and woods to work, it is often impossible to get medical attention at all. On one occasion when the writer was present as an employee, a crew of workmen were cutting timber in the forest ten miles away from camp. Two prisoners attempted escape during the noon hour. They were shot and killed by a guard. Had there been any possible means of summoning a physician, it might have been possible to save the life of one of them. The loss of blood, however, was too great and both died several hours later. In another case a young convict with but one year to serve attempted to escape and was shot in the leg. Since he had to be taken to the main highway on a wagon, the loss of blood was considerable and his leg had to be amputated.[8]

Few prisons have worse records than Parchman in its early history. The penitentiary has over the years, however, made many adaptations. Although a recent report of the

[8] Marvin Lee Hutson, "Mississippi's State Penal System" (Unpublished M. A. Thesis, University of Mississippi, 1939), 29.

Southern Regional Council labeled Parchman "brutal and archaic," [9] it is not the same today as it was when its image was established.

As it has developed, the penitentiary is a complex institution with what is for Mississippi a large budget. Its inmates grow their own food, make their own bedding and clothing, maintain the buildings, provide some of their own services, and grow nearly five thousand acres of cotton as well as many other crops. Cotton is the chief source of income, although profit is also derived from the sale of other crops as well as livestock. In an average year the institution is largely self-supporting. During the period from July 1, 1965 through June 30, 1967, for example, the total cash receipts from the penitentiary products were $2,342,-438, while the total prison expenses for the same period were $3,619,735.[10] Although products from the penitentiary are sold, the institution is financed by the state with all proceeds from the products being turned in to the state treasury.

Since Parchman operates as a plantation system, the buildings and other facilities at the penitentiary differ from those found at the average state prison in the United States. As its inmates say, Parchman is no "wall joint." There are no stone walls to match the popular image of a prison. One is well within the prison boundaries as he drives along U.S. Highway 49W before he sees anything

---

[9] Memphis *Commercial Appeal*, March 3, 1968.

[10] *Biennial Reports of the Superintendent and Other Officers of the Mississippi State Pententiary, July 1, 1964, through June 30, 1965,* p. 5.

to identify the fields on either side of the highway as prison property. In fact it is possible to drive through on the highway without seeing signs to distinguish Parchman from any other plantation in the area. The penitentiary buildings are similar to those of any other large cotton plantation and are of many different types: administration buildings, barns, storehouses, cotton gins, equipment sheds, and repair shops besides the dormitories housing the prisoners. The inmate camps which form the basic structure of the penitentiary are widely scattered, and only in these camps does Parchman take on the ordinary aspects of prison. The only fences are those which surround some of the individual camps. Unlike a prison such as Sing Sing in Ossining, New York, it is impossible to tour Parchman in one day. It is necessary to drive many miles around the plantation to see everything. The plantation is so large that a person can easily get lost if he is not familiar with it. In fact, he literally needs a roadmap to find his way from one part of the prison to another.

Each camp is a separate community within the plantation and is overseen by a sergeant responsible for the work of the camp as well as for discipline and order. Although separate and isolated, the camps work and play in competition with each other. The work of the plantation is allotted by camp and varies somewhat with the season of the year. The work may be planting, gathering, hog slaughtering, or whatever may be most urgently needed at any particular time. Since cotton is the major crop, much of the work for many inmates, especially in the fall, centers around its production. Like the other plantations in the

Delta, however, Parchman has begun to use machines for cotton picking, and not as many inmates have this duty now as in the past.

The penitentiary is controlled by a board of commissioners appointed by the governor. The board consists of five members, one of whom acts as chairman. Board members serve terms of four years each. State law requires that they be "outstanding citizens and qualified electors of the state of Mississippi," the only limitation being that none may be practicing attorneys.[11]

The commissioners, who review all activities of the penitentiary, are responsible for employing a general superintendent with authority over prison operations. The only legal requirements the commissioners have to meet in appointing a superintendent is to select "an experienced farmer of known executive ability."[12] Throughout its history, Parchman has been under the direction of men who could be described well by these qualifications. Although selected on a patronage basis, each man who became superintendent has been a good farmer who could operate the plantation well from an economic standpoint. Almost without exception, also, each has come into the penitentiary without any training in corrections. Even though some of the superintendents developed much concern for prison progress during their tenure as head of Parchman, a series of superintendents without training in corrections has been a severe handicap to the institution.

[11] *General Laws of Mississippi, 1960,* Chap. 284, paragraph 33, p. 402.
[12] *Ibid.*

It has made continuity in progressive programs difficult.

The commissioners also employ an assistant superintendent, a prison physician, an assistant physician, a dentist, a head nurse, assistant nurses, a head bookkeeper, a dispatch sergeant, and fifty guards, one of whom serves as captain.

The superintendent, in addition to hiring the necessary clerical personnel, is responsible for employing a farm manager whose duties include supervising all planning, planting, growing, cultivating, and harvesting of crops. Each phase of the penitentiary operation is under the immediate supervision of a sergeant. Thus the superintendent employs and supervises thirteen farm camp sergeants, as well as a gin sergeant, a dairy sergeant, an identification sergeant, a cold storage sergeant, a sergeant of the women's camp, seventeen first assistant sergeants, and seventeen second assistant sergeants.

The superintendent also employs a dietician mess sergeant who is required to go from one camp to another to supervise and plan the food menu in order to insure that the prisoners have balanced rations. Other service personnel who are employed by the superintendent include: X-ray and laboratory technicians; a laundry operator; a husbandman to supervise the dairy herd, beef herd, poultry, and hogs; a horticulturist; a chaplain; a classification officer; a records clerk; and an educational director. A complete breakdown of the employees and their salaries is given in Table 1.

All of the employees, except the physicians, live on the penitentiary grounds. The superintendent assigns each staff member housing for which rent of $7.50 a month is paid. This fee includes fuel, lights, and water charges. With the exception of the superintendent's house (a large, attractive brick home adjacent to the administration building), staff houses are of modest frame construction. They have the sameness in appearance as those found in textile mill towns of an earlier era in the South. Most of the staff houses are located near the administration area. The farm sergeants, however, live out near the camps they supervise. The penitentiary furnishes transportation to and from schools for the children of the employees. Each morning the penitentiary school bus picks up the children to deliver them to the schools of Drew, a town seven miles to the south.

Although the salaries of most positions at Parchman are low, staff members have fringe benefits which add to their real income. These include free medical attention and laundry service as well as commissary privileges. The commissary privilege saves staff members money on food, particularly meat. They are able to buy meats at approximately one-fourth the average retail price. Located near the administration building, Parchman's commissary looks much like a large country store. Almost any item found in a modern supermarket, however, may be purchased in the commissary by penitentiary staff members.

Although the outside world has little noted it, Parchman has recently taken long strides into modern correctional practice. Mechanized equipment has reduced much of the hand labor and replaced most of the six hundred mules used as recently as 1965.

Table 1

MISSISSIPPI STATE PENITENTIARY EMPLOYEES

Number of Employees	Position	Annual Salary*
1	Superintendent	$12,500
1	Asst. Superintendent	10,800
1	Secretary to Superintendent	4,500
1	Secretary	3,480
1	Office Manager	10,800
1	Accountant	5,760
1	Accountant	6,000
1	Head Bookkeeper	4,320
1	Property Officer	4,800
1	Purchasing Agent	6,600
1	School Bus Driver	1,500
2	Postal Clerks	3,240
1	Commissary Clerk	4,680
1	Asst. Commissary Clerk	3,060
1	Commissary Supply Truck Officer	3,240
6	Asst. Bookkeeper	3,240
1	General Maintenance	7,200
1	Canteen Supervisor	4,320
1	Canteen Assistant	3,900
1	Canteen Clerk	3,000
1	Classification Officer	6,600
1	Stenographer	4,080
1	Record Clerk	3,240
1	Chaplain	6,000
1	Asst. Chaplain	5,700
1	Security Administrator	5,700
1	Dispatch Sgt.	5,400
1	Security Officer-Captain of Guards	4,440

*Salary figures as of November, 1968.

Table 1 cont.

MISSISSIPPI STATE PENITENTIARY EMPLOYEES

Number of Employees	Position	Annual Salary
2	Guards	4,200
17	Guards	3,300
7	Maximum Security Unit Guards	3,420
23	Nightwatchmen	3,180
1	Music & Recreation Director	4,800
1	Prison Dentist	14,000
1	Head Nurse	4,200
3	Asst. Nurse	3,000
1	Identification Sgt.	4,800
1	Farm Manager	11,000
11	Camp Sgts.	4,440
6	Camp Sgts.	4,800
19	Drivers	3,480
1	Cold Storage Sgt.	4,440
1	Asst. Cold Storage Sgt.	4,200
1	Building Maintenance Sgt.	4,800
2	1st Asst. Sgts.	4,200
1	2nd Asst. Sgts.	3,600
1	Machine Shop Foreman	6,840
1	Asst. Machine Shop Foreman	5,400
1	Laundry Sgt.	3,600
1	Field Crop Supervisor	6,300
1	Asst. Field Crop Supervisor	4,440
1	Animal Husbandman	7,800
1	Horticulturist	6,600
1	Asst. Horticulturist	3,480
1	Beef Cattle Assistant	5,400
1	Hog Unit Sgt.	4,440

Table 1 cont.

MISSISSIPPI STATE PENITENTIARY EMPLOYEES

Number of Employees	Position	Annual Salary
1	Mills Mgr. & Rd. Maintenance	3,900
1	Poultry Sgt.	3,480
1	Gin Sgt.	7,200
1	Gen. Farm Mechanic	5,400
1	Machinery Supervisor	3,480
1	Road Sgt.	3,180
1	Road Sgt.	3,900
1	Part-time Physician (Camp B)	1,800
Vocational School & Bookbindery Salaries aggregate salary total for 18 employees		$118,200

Along with the changes in agricultural production, changes have occurred in the treatment of prisoners. Inmates at Parchman are now able to benefit from a wide range of training. In the early part of 1965, a vocational-educational program with fourteen different trade schools was put into effect. This training complex was completed at a cost of approximately $500,000 and includes training in welding, diesel and automotive mechanics, carpentry, and brick masonry. In the same year a library was installed with a central unit in the administration building, and books are now available at all camps on regular rotation. In 1966 a book binding plant was put into operation. It handles all binding for the Mississippi Text Book Commission, the State Library, and many educational institutions in the state. This facility is equipped to handle 25,000 books per year, and in addition to offering vocational training, saves the state approximately $100,000 annually.

Although Parchman's vocational and technical training programs are still new, many graduates from them are working at productive jobs on the outside. The Employment Security Commission helps locate jobs for prisoners who complete vocational courses.

The summer of 1968 marked the beginning operation of a reception and diagnostic center where incoming prisoners are given a series of tests and examinations before being assigned jobs. The full-time staff at the center includes a university graduate with a major in psychology and a counselor aide. These staff members are under the direction of two psychologists at Delta State College in Cleveland who spend two days a week at the penitentiary. In the diagnostic center, personality inventories, intelligence tests, and achievement tests are administered. A case history is also developed on each inmate. In the early days, penitentiary records showed only an inmate's race, his crime, and the length of his sentence.

On January 1, 1967, the inmates stopped wearing traditional prison stripes. They now wear blue denim shirts and trousers made by the female prisoners. Two full-time counselors have been employed to advise inmates immediately prior to their paroles or discharges. This period of counseling is not vocational; it seeks to help prepare the prisoner psychologically for his return to free society. In the winter the penitentiary operates an elementary school for inmates under the supervision of the educational director. The educational program is directed primarily toward those who are unable to read and write or those who have completed only a few years of schooling. Students are given one-half day off from work, five days a week to attend school. Teachers come from nearby communities in cooperation with the Adult Education Division of the State Department of Education, but some prisoners also serve in this capacity. Civil Defense classes are offered as an educational service for both inmates and members of the staff.

Parchman permits inter-camp sports which promote considerable rivalry between the camps. Baseball games and boxing matches are hotly contested seasonal sports, and winning teams are given trophies and prizes. A monthly newspaper called *Inside World* is written and edited solely by the prisoners and sponsored by the educational director. An inmate in each camp serves as a correspondent for the publication, which features news items, editorials, and a classified section in which prisoners advertise. The paper is distributed to all inmates and has an outside subscription list of about a thousand.

The educational director selects the movies which are shown every two weeks in each camp. He is also responsible for directing musical contests among inmates. Two prison bands, the Insiders and the Confiners, play at some camp every night. The bands serve as vocational training in addition to entertainment. Several band members have joined professional musical groups upon their release from Parchman.

Discipline at Parchman is primarily the responsibility of the individual camp sergeant, although there are peni-

tentiary rules which he must follow. If a prisoner becomes
unruly, there are three courses of action the sergeant may
take. The first of these, and probably the most frequently
used, is the withdrawal of privileges such as movies, recreational games, or television viewing. A second method of
discipline open to the sergeant is the transfer of the inmate
to the Maximum Security unit cell block. The sergeant
may have a prisoner placed here for a day, a week, or until
he indicates by his attitude and behavior a willingness to
abide by the rules in the regular camp. If a prisoner gives
trouble while in Maximum Security, he is kept for twenty-
four hours in a completely dark cell furnished only with
a toilet. He is fed but the food is prepared without salt
and other seasonings and is tasteless. Before current regulations were passed, prisoners have been held in the "hole,"
as the dark cell is called, as long as sixty-four days.

A third course of action a sergeant may take is corporal
punishment. This form of discipline is the most carefully controlled of all forms, and according to Parchman
officials, it has not been used since 1964. The laws of the
state, however, still allow it. The following quotation de-
scribes the statutory regulations of corporal punishment
at Parchman:

> Corporal punishment of any kind shall not be administered
> to any convict, except on authority of the superintendent,
> or in his absence, the acting superintendent. Provided, how-
> ever, that when corporal punishment is administered to any
> convict, it shall be in the presence of the superintendent,
> or the assistant superintendent, or the chaplain. Whenever
> a sergeant or other employee of the penitentiary considers

it necessary that a convict be punished, he must make a written report of the offense committed by the convict, and in the event the superintendent or acting superintendent considers it necessary that such a convict should be given corporal punishment, he shall give written authority therefore directed to the sergeant or in his absence, the acting sergeant, designed to administer such punishment, specifying the number of licks or lashes, not to exceed ten (10) that may be afflicted. The report of the sergeant to the effect that such punishment has been administered shall be delivered to the superintendent and shall be placed in the files of the convict and shall become a part of the permanent record of such convict.

Any employee violating the provisions of this section shall be immediately dismissed; and any employee who shall violate the provision of this section shall be guilty of a felony, and upon conviction therefore, shall be punished by imprisonment in the State Penitentiary for a term of not less than one year nor more than five years.[13]

When corporal punishment is administered, it consists of being whipped with a black leather strap about four inches wide and four feet long. Inmates and staff members alike refer to the strap as "Black Annie" or "Bull Hide." The lash was the most common form of punishment during the 1930's. An assistant sergeant in 1935 described the offenses for which inmates were whipped at that time as follows:

There are many minor offenses governed by the lash. For instance, when prisoners are "counting-off," if the prisoners

[13] *Ibid.*

fail to give the correct count-number they are given five
lashes. Lack of efficiency in work often results in five lashes.
Disrespect to officers is punished by as many as fifteen
lashes. The administration of more than fifteen lashes is a
violation of penitentiary rules, and under no condition is
this done, unless the prisoner attempts to escape. In the
event that he is recaptured there is no limit as to the number of lashes administered. Any misconduct in the dining
room is punishable to the extent of five lashes. Getting out
of line during the count results in five lashes. Failure to
address an official correctly is punished to the extent of
five lashes also. If a prisoner fails to remove his hat as an
official passes by he is punished five lashes. During work
assignments if a prisoner fails to signal the trusty guard
when he wishes to be excused he is given five lashes.
Smoking while doing work details is also a five-lash offense.[14]

In describing his experiences, the same assistant sergeant
wrote:

The rules are accepted as matters of fact by the convicts,
and they often converse good-naturedly with the driver
[assistant sergeant] about the lash. Prisoners sometimes
offer the driver five lashes if, for example, he would let them
smoke a cigarette during work assignments. During the
employ of the writer as a driver, a prisoner approached him
with an offer of five lashes if he would be granted permission to fish in an adjoining canal for thirty minutes. The
free attitude which characterizes the majority of negroes
at Parchman is only a manifestation of the recognized typical rural negro in the South. Prisoners in the State Peniten-

[14] Hutson, "Mississippi's State Penal System," 22.

tiary do not live in constant dread of the lash by any means. This is true to a considerable extent among negro prisoners. On the other hand white prisoners are more prone to at-attempt escape as a result of their dread of the lash.[15]

Many of the long-term staff members at Parchman still favor the lash. Following a riot in one of the camps in January of 1968, a legislative committee reported that a number of sergeants recommended the lash be used again as a means of solving disciplinary problems. One sergeant, for example, told the committee that he was in favor of using the lash. "A little of the strap goes a long way," he said. Another believed the lash more effective for trouble-some prisoners than letting them "live it up" in Maximum Security. "The strap on them would be the best thing that ever happened," he said. "I admit the strap has been abused at times," he added, "but if I had a son up here I would rather see him get his hide tanned than to be put in Maximum Security." [16]

It would not be without precedent if whipping were to be reinstituted. The lash was not used from 1960 until early in 1963 when it was reinstated, used frequently during that summer and fall, and then discontinued again early in 1964. At the time that the lash was reinstated, Tom Ross, a prison commissioner, said that without it the prisoners were weighing in after a day's work with only about fifty pounds of cotton. But with the lash again being used, he said they were picking up to three hundred

[15] *Ibid.*, 230.

[16] Both sergeants are quoted in Baton Rouge *State-Times,* February 2, 1968.

pounds a day. Superintendent C. E. Breazeale, a graying, pipe-smoking man with the air of a kindly schoolmaster, expressed his attitude toward the lash in March of 1963 as follows: "We didn't seem to get the job done without it. We're getting along fine now." [17]

It does not seem likely, however, that the lash will be employed frequently in the future. The changes that have occurred at Parchman since 1964 are not compatible with it. Many of the staff members take pride in the progressive steps they have made and look upon the lash as outmoded. This is especially true of the younger staff members. The penitentiary is currently in the midst of change. There is a struggle between the old and the new, but the old patterns do not change quickly. Parchman is still a tough prison where inmates work long hours under the gun. However, inroads have been made, such as the rehabilitation programs, and long-term prisoners say that Parchman is not at all like the place they remember at the beginning of their sentences.

As previously mentioned, the organizational framework of the penitentiary is formed around a series of semi-autonomous camps located at various places throughout the plantation. The camps are racially segregated, although the new vocational programs are integrated. In the prefabricated steel buildings erected for vocational training, Negroes and whites attend classes side by side and eat together in the school's cafeteria. At night they return to segregated camps.

Each camp has one main structure—a large rectangular

[17] "Black Annie," *Newsweek,* March 18, 1963, p. 33.

central building for the detention of prisoners. The buildings called "cages," are built and maintained by prison labor. They are one-story brick structures, designed so that an average of sixty inmates may be housed in one wing. In each wing there are no partitions or cells separating the prisoners. They are housed in congregate quarters with electric lights, lavatories, showers, and toilet facilities. Some of the camp buildings are surrounded by wire fences; most are not. Whether a camp has a fence around it depends mostly on its location. Those located out on the plantation generally do not; camps located near the highway usually do.

The inmates sleep in beds arranged about two or three feet apart in the pattern of a military barracks. In all but one or two camps, the beds are single-deckers. Each inmate keeps his personal property in a locker under his bed. Each wing is ventilated by about ten windows covered by bars. A hall, dividing the wings of each camp building, leads to a central dining room which also serves as an educational and recreational room where movies are shown. Trusties, who do much of the guarding of prisoners at Parchman, have separate quarters in each camp building.

Trusties are appointed by the sergeants and comprise about 20 percent of the inmate population. Not all trusties are guards. Those chosen for guard duty are usually men with long sentences who have earned special respect and trust from the sergeants. Trusties are disciplined in much the same way as prisoners in the ranks. If a trusty is charged with a minor offense, he may be punished and keep his rank. He may, however, have his position as a trusty removed and then earn it back again through good behavior. Trusties who do not guard prisoners are used as cooks or servants for the staff members or they are placed in jobs where they are not guarded. Camp sergeants are in charge of prisoners during work assignments. They are helped by the assistant sergeants, called "drivers," who see that work details are carried out. Trusty guards are called "shooters." They carry .38 caliber Winchester rifles and stand guard over the prisoners as they work. Prisoners are never under the control of trusty guards alone.

Each camp has a concession stand attended by an inmate appointed by the sergeant of the camp. Each wing of the "cage" also has a television set which the inmates may watch in their free hours if they choose. A night watchman (a civilian guard under the supervision of the sergeant) is assigned to the sleeping quarters of the prisoners. He is assisted by a "cage man," as the trusty guard on night duty is known, who checks the prisoners into their sleeping quarters. There is a cage man on duty in each of the wings during the night. Before he is dismissed from duty, the night watchman must check all prisoners out of their quarters with the sergeant or one of the drivers.

A kitchen in which trusty cooks prepare the food is connected with each camp's dining room. Each prisoner is allowed three-fourths of a pound of meat a day, a quart of milk, and all the bread and vegetables he wants. Even during the days that Parchman operated only as a profit-making plantation the convicts had plenty of wholesome food. They were fed well because they could not work efficiently if they were not healthy. Since all of the food is grown on the plantation, officials do not have to worry about its cost.

Adjacent to each camp building is a storeroom containing work equipment and gun racks where the rifles used for guarding prisoners during the day are locked at night. The sergeant of each camp has possession of the storeroom keys. A guard stand is in front of each camp. All visitors must be cleared here by a civilian guard before they enter the camp area. To the rear of each male camp, except for Maximum Security, stands the "red house," the building to which a married inmate may take his wife when she comes to visit him.

The grounds around each camp are landscaped. Grass and trees grow in the yards, and frequently flowers. Most camps have picnic areas with tables which the prisoners and their visitors use when the weather is favorable. Some camps have play equipment for children accompanying the visitors. The main building in each camp has a covered porch across the front where inmates and visitors may retire when the weather is inclement.

The individual camps are organized and located in a manner following the particular productive, maintenance, or service functions which they fulfill in the operation of the institution as a whole. Twelve camps are identified simply by number. Others are known as Camp B, Women's Camp, Front Camp, the Dairy Unit, Maximum Security, First Offenders, and the Hospital. Table 2 shows the number of prisoners in each. A brief description of each camp and its organization function follows:

Table 2

TOTAL INMATE POPULATION BY CAMP, OCTOBER 29, 1968

Camps	Number
Camp One	140
Camp Two	137
Camp Three	77
Camp Four	73
Camp Five	94
Camp Six	113
Camp Seven	72
Camp Eight	105
Camp Nine	74
Camp Ten	144
Camp Eleven	89
Camp Twelve	0
Camp B	124
Women's Camp	39
Front Camp	68
Dairy	27
Hospital	61
Maximum Security	14
First Offenders	99
Whitfield State Hospital	23
Governor's Mansion	9
Total	1,582

Camp One is located directly across the highway in front and east of the administration building and the superintendent's home. This is a Negro camp, enclosed by a wire fence because of its proximity to the highway. The men in this unit are mostly first offenders. They do general farm work devoted mainly to 224 acres of cotton. However, the men share in the harvesting of corn on the plantation as well. Like most of the other camps, this unit has a portion of its acreage allotted to the growing of vegetables. Many men from Camp One are also enrolled in vocational training.

Camp Two contains the Negro prisoners who are assigned to limited physical work duty and is located one and a half miles west of the administration building. Many of the men housed here, however, are not physically disabled. The unit is engaged primarily in growing vegetables. Having no cotton acreage alloted to them, these men are responsible for slaughtering the hogs grown on the plantation.

Camp Three is a Negro general farming camp located on the southern border of the penitentiary. The inmates of the camp till 485 acres of cotton as well as large amounts of corn, soy beans, and sugar cane. A 12-acre lake is near the camp building.

Camp Four houses the disabled white prisoners, although, as in the case of the Negro disability camp, many of its men are physically sound. The camp is responsible for a limited amount of farm work centering around 73 acres of cotton. The chief enterprises located here are the institutional laundry and the greenhouse which supplies plants for the penitentiary.

Camp Five is situated about one mile southwest of the administration area. One of the larger camps (usually housing about 150 white men), it is surrounded by a wire fence and has picnic areas. The men of this unit plant, cultivate, and gather nearly 700 acres of cotton as well as other crops. The inmate newspaper is published in a building on the grounds of this camp. A detail of men also breed and train bloodhounds to be used by the penitentiary and other state agencies.

Camp Six is near the center of the Parchman plantation. Enclosed by a fence, the unit houses white men who do general farm work. The grounds around the camp have three picnic areas with tables and benches. The prisoners in Camp Six are chiefly occupied with the cultivation of 665 acres of cotton.

Camp Seven is located west of Camp Six and north of Camp Four. It has no fence. Camp Seven was closed in January of 1967, and its Negro inmates were sent to other camps. In the summer of 1968, this unit was converted into a reception and diagnostic center. In the past, the inmates have grown nearly 500 acres of cotton each season. Details of men in the camp have bred and grown the work stock used on the plantation in past years.

Camp Eight usually houses about 150 Negro men who do general farm work. Located on the northwest border of Parchman, the camp is often allotted over 600 acres of cotton as well as many acres of corn, soy beans, and vegetables.

Camp Nine is a white camp usually having only twenty or thirty men. This unit is an honor camp situated about two miles east of Camp Eight. The inmates who are assigned here are selected not only for good behavior but also for the skills they possess. They do the carpentry work, painting, building repairs, plumbing, and construction for the penitentiary. Their work, consequently, necessitates their moving from camp to camp. Camp Nine is among the most attractive in appearance, having a small lake with picnic areas, flowers, and trees on its grounds.

Camp Ten is a Negro camp. The central building stands two miles east of Camp Nine. The men of this unit care for 380 acres of cotton as well as other crops. It includes among its inmates the "hog unit," a group of men, under a separate sergeant, who care for the 2,900 swine bred and grown in the penitentiary in a typical year.

Camp Eleven is the northernmost of the camps on the Parchman plantation and has a capacity for nearly 200 prisoners. It is a Negro camp. The men grow 368 acres of cotton, and also corn, soy beans, and vegetables.

Camp Twelve was closed in May of 1967 as the inmate population at Parchman has decreased in recent years. It is being retained as a regular camp, however, in the event that it is needed again. The inmates are engaged in general farming when the camp is in operation.

Camp B is the most isolated of all. It is a Negro camp about twenty-five miles north of Parchman near the Lambert community. Camp B is composed of 6,000 acres of land, 4,500 of which are devoted to timber. The men here cultivate and harvest 269 acres of cotton, and 200 acres of rice. A sawmill is located here and accounts for a considerable amount of the workload of the camp. It also provides lumber used in the construction of penitentiary buildings.

Front Camp does not usually contain over fifty men. It

is an unfenced camp for white men and is located back of the administration building near the cotton gin. The men of this camp work as clerks in the commissary, as electricians, machinists, mechanics, telephone operators, linemen, and maintenance men, and operate the cotton gin and the shoe shop. These prisoners are also selected for good behavior as well as for skills necessary for the jobs they do.

Women's Camp houses both white and Negro women in quarters separated by a driveway. Situated between Camp Two and the Front Camp, the unit generally has about fifty or sixty women who operate the plantation cannery which produces about 130,000 gallons of vegetables and fruit annually. In addition the women make the mattresses, inmate clothing, pillows, sheets, and all other items produced by sewing.

Dairy Unit is a Negro camp located near the Women's Camp. It is small, usually composed of around thirty inmates who care for the dairy herd consisting of 503 head of cattle including 266 mature milch cows. The men sent to this camp have also been selected for their good behavior.

Hospital is an accredited sixty-five-bed general service hospital approved and licensed under the name of Sunflower Hospital. It is located behind and near Camp Two. The hospital is staffed by one full-time general practitioner, a surgeon in attendance three afternoons a week, a dermatologist one day a month, and one graduate nurse, one licensed practical nurse, and one nurse's aide, all fulltime. It serves the staff of the institution as well as the inmates. (Although the inmates of Camp B use the hospital in cases of surgery or hospitalization, a private physician in nearby Marks is employed to take care of routine sick call cases at this camp.) A complete physical examination and laboratory work-up, including a serological test for syphilis, is given to each inmate prior to his assignment to a camp. A regular sick call schedule has been established for each camp to facilitate the treatment of nonemergency cases. The hospital also includes the dental clinic which offers routine and emergency treatment for inmates and staff. Parchman doctors also refer patients to the University Medical Center in Jackson and utilize the services of the other medical facilities supported by the state, including the Mississippi State Hospital at Whitfield for diagnosis and treatment in suspected and known mental cases.

Maximum Security is located about halfway between the hospital and the administration building. This camp does not fit into the general pattern of the other camps at Parchman. Surrounded by a high fence, including a guard tower, Maximum Security is entered through electrically controlled gates. The unit contains cells for inmates convicted of capital crimes and sentenced to death. The gas chamber is attached to the rear of the building. Men sent from the regular camps for disciplinary reasons are held here. The number of inmates in Maximum Security is never large. Ordinarily, the number varies between fifteen and twenty.

First Offenders' Camp is the newest of the inmate camps, having opened in June of 1965. It is a large brick unit without a fence built on the same pattern as the other camps. Its grounds include a chapel. This camp contains youthful white inmates, most of whom are serving their first sentences in an adult institution. Although the men here do general farm work, a large number of them are involved in the vocational and rehabilitation programs recently instituted at the penitentiary.

Although the individual camps remain the core of Parchman's organization, with the exception of Maximum Security they are becoming more uniform in equipment and programs. Plans are in progress for the building of a large unified recreational facility which will include a swimming pool, tennis courts, baseball fields, and a rodeo arena. The recreation center, however, will still emphasize the individual camps. Most of the activities in the center will consist of competitive sports featuring contests between teams from the separate camps.

The entire penitentiary is undergoing almost constant change. The picture at Parchman resembles that of the state as a whole in that new emphasis is being placed upon the development of industrial skills. However, agriculture still plays a vital role and remains the chief support of the penitentiary. It will probably continue to do so in the foreseeable future. Parchman's agricultural economy, however, is much more diversified than it used to be. Cotton may still be king, but truck crops are steadily increasing in acreage.

Consequently, Parchman is a mixture of the old and the new. One may find here practices which range from the modern to the archaic. Along with one of the finest vocational-industrial schools in corrections, one sees prison inmates working the "long line" from daylight to dark very much as they did fifty years ago. A visitor at Parchman, however, gets the impression that rehabilitation is now being emphasized. The attitude of the current superintendent, Thomas D. Cook, who began his job early in 1968, symbolizes the new at the penitentiary. A vigorous young man with progressive ideas and plans, Cook considers his job exciting and is dedicated to continued development within the institution. "It's easy to punish a man for his crime," Cook said in October, 1968, "but the possibility of returning him to society as a responsible citizen offers a real challenge. . . . We are making every effort to cut down on the number of men who come back to prison because they can't make it in the outside world." [18]

[18] Memphis *Commercial Appeal,* October 1, 1968.

Chapter II

The Conjugal Visit

Every other Sunday is visiting day at the Mississippi State Penitentiary. Although visiting hours do not begin until one o'clock in the afternoon, the visitors begin arriving at any time after midmorning. Most arrive in private automobiles, although some come by bus or taxi. Visiting hours end at five o'clock. From the time Parchman was established up until 1966, visitors were allowed every Sunday afternoon for two hours. For the past three years, however, they have been limited to every other week. The length of time inmates and their visitors may spend with each other has remained the same—four hours every two weeks.

Until the visiting hours start, the visitors wait in their cars parked on the sides of the highway between Camp One and the administration building. As the time draws near, they drive in the main entrance and clear with a guard who inspects the car and records the number of the license plate. The visitors then drive by the administration building, past the hospital, and out on the plantation to the camp that houses the inmate they wish to visit.

Upon arrival at the camp, the visitors must undergo another inspection by the camp sergeant or the guard on duty at the entrance to the grounds. This inspection is more rigid than that at the main entrance to the penitentiary, particularly if it is the first time the visitor has appeared at the camp. The visitors must identify themselves and, if requested, submit to being searched. Usually, however, a visual inspection is all that occurs. The guard looks into the car and the car trunk, records the visitors' names, and if the visiting hours have begun, admits them into the camp area and informs the prisoner concerned that he has visitors. The prisoner then is allowed to come out of the camp building unguarded, receive his guests, and visit with them unsupervised within the camp area.

The penitentiary allows all members of a prisoner's family to visit him, except in the case where a member of the family has been previously incarcerated in Parchman. The institution does not allow released inmates to return for visits with other inmates; consequently, a member of one's own family may not visit if the member himself has formerly been sentenced to Parchman. Otherwise, however, members of a prisoner's family are encouraged to visit him on every occasion which they can manage. For a married man, the visiting freedom means that he may see his wife in private, and have sexual relations with her.

The conjugal visit at Parchman should not be viewed as an isolated phenomenon occurring in an institution otherwise following the same practices as other penal institutions in the United States. Parchman has the most liberal visitation and leave programs of any state penitentiary in the nation. The conjugal visit should be seen in this perspective for it is only a part of a general program in which family contacts for inmates are emphasized. The institution is not only liberal in permitting visitors, but also allows an inmate to maintain contact with his family by leaving the prison himself. As late as 1958, Parchman was the only American penal institution which permitted inmates to make home visits for reasons other than emergency.[1] Convicts who have served at least three years with good behavior records are regularly granted ten-day-furloughs under the Holiday Suspension program each year from December 1 to March 1. The staff feels that this program has been highly successful and is an important factor in inmate morale. In an average year approximately 300 prisoners are given furloughs. Since the prison population is down now, not as many are released. In 1961, 578 were given furloughs; in 1962, 462; in 1965, 301. During 1967, out of 219 taking leaves under the Holiday Suspension program, only 2 did not return voluntarily.

A few other prison systems in the United States have recently developed work-release programs in which inmates are permitted to work at civilian jobs outside prison walls during the day. And many other penitentiaries have instituted furlough programs similar to the one in existence at Parchman. For instance, in the neighboring state of Louisiana, a system of granting Christmas furloughs to inmates of all the state's adult correctional institutions was begun in 1964 and has been expanding ever since. Well over 200 inmates went home for Christmas in 1968 and all returned on schedule. The Louisiana criteria for the selection of prisoners to receive the furloughs is that they be good security risks (no drug addicts or sex criminals, etc.) and that they have good behavioral records.[2]

[1] Zemans and Cavan, "Marital Relationships for Prisoners," 50–57.
[2] Information received from Mr. Robert Rochester, penologist for the Louisiana State Department of Institutions.

While Mississippi prison officials believe that furloughs are also important in maintaining family relationships and wholesome inmate attitudes, the family visit is emphasized at Parchman and the conjugal visit seems a logical part of it. The conjugal visit has developed informally, and it is still best described as an informal, unofficial program. That is to say, when the practice began cannot be determined from the existing penitentiary records. It still does not have legal status or control. In fact, until the First Offenders' Camp was built in 1963, funds were not allocated for the construction of the buildings or red houses used in the program. Records are not kept as to which inmates have conjugal visits, nor does an inmate have to make application for the privilege or hold any particular grade as an inmate.

There was no employee at Parchman interviewed during the time of this study whose memory went back to a time before conjugal visits were allowed. Most of the employees believed that the practice had been in existence, in some form, since the penitentiary was first opened in its present location. One man, who had been employed there intermittently for over thirty-five years and who lived near the penitentiary and had knowledge of it even before his employment, said that conjugal visits were allowed as long ago as 1918.

Although the practice has been in existence for many years, it has only developed into a somewhat systematic program within the last ten or fifteen years. In the early days it was apparently confined to the Negro camps, and there were few if any controls. A man who was employed

at the penitentiary in 1935 described the practice at that
time as follows:

> An interesting but unique feature of the penitentiary system
> is in dealing with the races. As for example, no visitors of
> any type are allowed in the living quarters for white men
> unless they are chaperoned. Yet truck loads of women are
> permitted to enter the various camps for Negro men. Com-
> mercial prostitutes make their weekly visits to these camps
> and are permitted without any type of examination.
> Another interesting feature with regard to such actions, is
> that quarters are provided for these Negro women during
> their visits to the camps. During the day they occupy rooms
> on the basement floor of the central building. It was im-
> possible for the writer, during the time of his employment,
> to obtain a definite reason for this unusual racial differ-
> ence.[3]

No one recalls just when the first building for conjugal
visits was constructed. It is probable, however, that none
were in existence very long before 1940. The sergeant of
a Negro camp said, for example, that when he became
sergeant of his camp in 1940 conjugal visits were allowed
but no facilities were provided for them. The usual thing,
he related, was for the inmates to take their wives or girl
friends into the prisoners' sleeping quarters and secure
whatever privacy they could by hanging up blankets. Upon
gaining control of his camp, the sergeant allowed the inmates to construct a building for conjugal visits and has
continued to allow the construction of buildings or addi-
tions to the existing ones. At the time the sergeant was in-

[3] Hutson, "Mississippi's State Penal System," 48.

terviewed, his camp had three conjugal visiting houses, each containing several rooms. He also said he had no idea whether or not his camp was the first to have houses for conjugal visits. However, as his is one of the isolated camps, the sergeant stated that he didn't know much about the practice in the other camps, especially when he first came to the penitentiary.

The buildings provided for the conjugal visits are referred to by the inmates and staff as "red houses." No employee at Parchman remembers the specific origin of this term. Apparently, one of the first buildings provided for the purpose was painted red and the inmates spoke of it as the red building or house. Most of the red houses are of simple frame construction and contain about five or six rooms, although some have as many as ten. In each room there is a bed and a table, and in some a mirror. There is a bathroom in each red house.

Since the red houses have been built in an unsystematic and unplanned manner, they are not standard in appearance, nor do they have the quality of workmanship found in the other buildings. They do not, on the average, make an attractive appearance. Most have been built as inconspicuously as possible behind other buildings. The red houses have, since 1960, begun to show improvement, particularly in the last three or four years. Almost every sergeant interviewed mentioned a feature of the red house in his camp to which he himself had contributed. One mentioned a new roof, while others spoke of painting, adding new rooms, or acquiring new furnishings.

The only conjugal visiting facilities at Parchman

planned and specifically provided for by the penitentiary are those at the First Offenders' Camp opened in 1965. The planning and construction of the conjugal visiting facilities at this camp denote a significant advance in the institutional acceptance of the privilege of conjugal visiting at Parchman. Prior to the construction of the First Offenders' Camp, all conjugal visiting facilities were constructed through the informal, accommodative relationships between the individual camp sergeant and his men. The inmates would request permission to build a facility and the sergeant would allow them to do so. The buildings were constructed out of whatever scrap lumber and other materials the inmates and sergeants could secure. In the First Offenders' Camp, however, the red house was included in the camp plan from the beginning and it is made of the same brick and other materials as the main building itself. The main camp building is beside a chapel, and a few yards to the rear of the two is the red house. The rooms in this building afford privacy equal to the rooms in a modern motel, though they are by comparison rather spartan.

The entire conjugal visiting program at Parchman should, in fact, be considered still in a developmental stage. It is likely that the program has just now begun to take on the pattern that it will have in the future. Although it has been in existence for many years without official recognition, the staff members have recently begun to speak freely of the practice among themselves—and to speak of it with frankness and pride.

Even though the program has begun to be recognized

and supported, informality has been retained in the operation of the conjugal visit at Parchman. The inmate and his
wife are given as little surveillance as possible. They are
not asked to fill out papers or to make any formal application to use the privilege. Inmates are neither encouraged
nor discouraged as to the use of the privilege. The decision
is for the couple to make. Wives are not informed in any
official way that they are allowed to make conjugal visits.
The individual inmate is responsible for informing his
wife of the privilege and answering any questions she may
have about it. The individual camp sergeant is, however,
responsible for checking the wife's presentation of a marriage license or other identifying document when she
enters the camp area on visiting days.

The penitentiary provides no contraceptive devices for
the inmates, nor is their use required. If an inmate and his
wife wish to use contraceptives the wife must provide
them. The attitude of the penitentiary staff toward the
conjugal visiting privilege is simply to leave the inmate
and his wife alone and let them have complete privacy.
After a brief inspection for contraband materials, the inmate's wife is allowed into the camp area where she is
greeted by her husband. The family visit may begin with
a picnic lunch. The inmate and his wife are free to walk
around the camp grounds and select a spot for the family
picnic away from anyone else. The grounds around each
camp building are extensive enough to allow inmates and
their visitors to be considerably removed from any other
inmates or staff members. When the weather is warm, the
grounds around a camp building, although perhaps less

crowded, look somewhat like a city park on a Sunday afternoon. People sit on blankets eating picnic lunches; others sit on benches in the shade of trees. One may even see a boy and his father having a game of catch with a baseball, or children playing by themselves.

The penitentiary imposes as little as possible upon the privacy of inmates and their visitors. Once the guests have passed the preliminary screening, they are not approached by a staff member until the inspection upon leaving—unless an inmate and his wife wish to talk to a staff member during the visit, which they sometimes do. The time in between the initial and final inspection is unsupervised; a visit as nearly unrestricted as possible is the goal of the penitentiary officials. Since the practice of conjugal visiting at Parchman has received some public notice, newspaper and magazine reporters have wanted to take pictures of visiting day at Parchman. The penitentiary staff, however, has not allowed this as a rule for they believe it would violate the rights of privacy.

To a person familiar only with the typical American penal institution, the freedom of visiting at Parchman seems unbelievable. One must remember, however, that the Mississippi State Penitentiary is in fact a large plantation. There are over twelve acres of land for each inmate—more space than many institutions have for a total population of several hundred. The penitentiary is isolated and situated on flat terrain, and supervision may be effective even though the officers are a hundred yards from the people they watch. One does not have to worry about inmates hiding in corridors or slipping over walls, for these do not exist. The main thing a guard has to do is watch the "gun line" around the camp which the prisoners may not cross.[4] As long as they stay within the gun lines, the prisoners may move about freely. If an inmate decided to run off, he would have to run for several miles in plain view over flat, cleared land before he could find a hiding place. In such a location, with inmates divided into camps, a penal institution does not have to emphasize security for the terrain itself provides it. With bloodhounds following him, a prisoner stands almost no chance of getting away. As one staff member said: "If a man breaks, we usually just bust a couple of caps [shoot a couple of times] over his head and let him run. These dogs are good and they like to run. Anyway, a man would have to run all the way to Clarksdale to get away." The majority of prisoners who escape from Parchman are trusties who slip away from an isolated work assignment where they have been placed alone.

The freedom and informality of the conjugal visiting program are revealed by the fact that the inmates themselves are responsible for the orderly operation of the conjugal visiting buildings and for cooperation in the use of them. No limit is imposed by the staff on the length of time a prisoner and his wife may stay in the red house. The prisoners are left to use their own judgment. They are aware of how many inmates have wives visiting on a single day, and they understand that when fewer visitors come they may stay longer in the red house. Most of the sergeants are of the opinion that if the prisoners want the

---

[4] The "gun line" is an imaginary line around each camp and is marked only by small signposts spaced intermittently.

privilege they must participate in it without causing any problems. Expressing his attitude toward the privilege, a sergeant of a white camp remarked: "It works real smooth here. In fact, I don't have to bother with it myself. They keep the building clean and don't give me any headaches. My men know it's not allowed in other places and they appreciate it. I don't act any different about this privilege than I do about anything else. My men know I won't put up with any grab ass about anything. I just tell them to not try and shuck me and we will get along fine."

In camps having a fairly large number of men whose wives visit them, systems have been worked out by the inmates to avoid embarrassment in determining whether or not a room in the red house is being used. The usual procedure is to place a board in front of the building indicating which rooms are in use. Each room is numbered and its number is written on a separate marker. A string or chain is then attached to the marker and it is hung on the board. Before an inmate and his wife go into the building, they select a room, remove the marker from the board, and take it with them into the room. A later couple may then determine whether or not the red house has rooms available simply by walking past the board. This procedure prevents embarrassment arising over such things as knocking on doors, standing in line, and other incidents likely to be of concern.

In leaving the inmates alone without formal rules and regulations, the penitentiary forces them to cooperate with each other if they are to have the privilege. By informal agreement, married inmates whose wives are visiting them are left to themselves in one area of the camp grounds. Men who do not have wives or whose wives are not visiting them stay away from the area in which the red houses are located. Inmates may cooperate by watching or attending to the children of a couple in the red house. Above all, the men are respectful and courteous to each others' wives.

There are few restrictions on the inmates who make use of the conjugal visiting privileges. Those in the Maximum Security unit do not have the privilege, nor do women inmates. All married inmates in the other camps, however, have the privilege. No restrictions are imposed because of the nature of the crime committed by an inmate, nor for bad behavior for inmates not in the security unit. Nor does an inmate's wife have to have an examination for venereal diseases. As long as a married man meets the minimum expectations for inmates, he remains in a regular camp and is eligible for conjugal visits.

While there is always the understandable possibility that removal of the conjugal visiting privilege might be employed by the staff as a threat to keep inmates in line, it is not, and apparently has never been so used. The officials at Parchman believe that a man and his wife have the right of sexual intercourse even though the man is in prison. The small number of inmates found in Maximum Security at any one time indicates that removal of conjugal visiting privileges are not used as punishment. But since inmates who have this privilege value it highly, it is probably helpful in keeping inmates cooperative. It is difficult to ascertain the influence of the program on the overall behavior of inmates, however, since it is only one of many privileges which are allowed inmates in the regular camps.

Inmates are eligible to engage in conjugal visits after commitment as soon as they are assigned to a camp. No special counseling is given to an inmate using the privilege. He is treated like any other, except that he and his wife take part in the conjugal visiting program. The unselected and unrestricted use of the conjugal visiting privilege, while perhaps not in line with modern classification philosophy, does work to advantage for research purposes. Since inmates receiving conjugal visits are not selected for their good behavior or cooperative attitudes, any differences in their attitudes can be linked with this privilege. Whether or not an inmate takes advantage of the privilege depends entirely upon his own marital circumstances.

If a married inmate at Parchman does not use the privilege, it is generally because his wife does not live close enough to visit him, or because he and his wife are not getting along well, or because they simply do not choose to use it. Most married inmates not using the privilege or using it very rarely fall into the first category. In many cases, an inmate and his wife have not been getting along well before his incarceration. Inmates serving a sentence for nonsupport, for example, are often in this category. A few inmates reported that their wives engaged in conjugal visiting on the first incarceration but that on the prisoner's second commitment, the wives refused.

A small number of inmates do not use the privilege because they or their wives do not wish to do so. This may be because children, parents, and other members of the family come with the wife to visit. Or it may be because the inmate or his wife is embarrassed by the idea. More than half of the married inmates surveyed in 1963 took part in the program. Of 776 married inmates studied, 465 (59.9 percent) were receiving conjugal visits. Of the 465 men taking advantage of the privilege, 124 were white and 341 were Negro. The greater number of Negro men taking part in the program is accounted for mainly by the fact that Negroes in Parchman outnumber the whites by over 2 to 1. The smaller number of whites is also a reflection of the fact that more white inmates are from out of the state and their wives live farther away. Negroes, however, do not appear to participate more frequently in the program than the whites. In 1963, when visits could be made every Sunday, among both white and Negro men the average inmate received a conjugal visit once every two weeks. This pattern was the major consideration in the decision of penitentiary officials to allow visits only every other Sunday.

A more detailed analysis of the findings of the 1963 survey is presented in Chapter 5. It is interesting to note here, however, that the largest number of men taking advantage of the conjugal visiting privileges were Negroes over the age of twenty-five. Those prisoners receiving visits were more likely to be serving their first prison sentences (59 percent) than were those not receiving visits (55 percent). The men participating in the program also tended to be slightly better educated.

The fact that the average inmate who has his wife visit him and who uses the red house facilities tends to be slightly older than those inmates who don't is not of significant importance. Nor does it reflect any attitudinal differences. Rather, it is simply descriptive of the prison population at Parchman. Here, as is true in other adult correctional institutions in America, the largest segment of inmates is made up of young men not yet married. Consequently, prisoners receiving conjugal visits, being married, are older than the average inmate.

The difference in the educational level, however, is not so easily explained. Younger prisoners are generally better educated than the older ones, and therefore one would expect to find those receiving conjugal visits would have less education as they are older. One possible explanation may be the fact that since prostitutes are no longer admitted and marriage licenses are checked, only married men are eligible for conjugal visits. And recent studies have shown that, among married couples, the better educated are less inhibited by the old Puritanical mores and are therefore more willing to have sexual relations under varying conditions.[5] The men at Parchman who receive conjugal visits are perhaps following this pattern.

However, the most likely difference, and the most important, between the inmates who have conjugal visits from their wives and those who do not is a viable marriage. The survey and interviews of 1963 plainly indicate the fact that, as the program is now set up at Parchman, the most necessary factor to its success is that a prisoner have a wife who is interested in him and his welfare and who lives close enough to visit him.

[5] William H. Masters and Virginia E. Johnson, *Human Sexual Response* (Boston, 1966), Chap. 2.

Chapter III

Why Conjugal Visiting in Mississippi?

Since conjugal visiting is so unusual in American penology, it is important to consider how it could develop and operate in a Mississippi prison. Such a liberal practice would seem to be inconsistent with the conservative image Mississippi usually presents. Furthermore, the Mississippi State Penitentiary has for most of its history been known as a "tough" prison where inmates did their time with little hope for parole. One would expect that if conjugal visiting developed anywhere in the United States, it would do so in a prison with a philosophy of rehabilitation and treatment and in a state noted for liberal developments.

Conjugal visiting in Mississippi has consequently been regarded both popularly and professionally as a prison program inconsistent with the cultural unit and social order in which it is located. As a matter of fact, however, the structure and organization of the Mississippi State Penitentiary have been factors in the development of the conjugal visit, and the practice is consistent with other elements in Mississippi's social system. This is to say, general features of the state and specific aspects of its prison are especially amenable to conjugal visiting even though the practice is not accepted in other American prisons. The rural environment in which the penitentiary is located, the plantation life it follows, the small semi-isolated camps which characterize the institution, its economic motives, and the segregation of the Negro and white races within the prison—all these features have been significant in the development of conjugal visiting. And as a functioning program it is dependent upon them.

Although a prison is popularly thought of as an institution existing in isolation from civilian norms and values, in reality the objectives and policies of correctional institutions are largely reflections of beliefs and values extant in the broader community supporting and surrounding them. In American society especially, civilian influences on the activities of correctional administrators are strong because most prison officials regard themselves as representatives of the state under whose authority the inmates are held. Since most prisons depend upon legislatures for financial support, prison officials carry a public trust and their duties and responsibilities are to a large extent defined for them in terms of law as well as by the conventional beliefs held in the larger community. If their objectives deviate very far from those of the community, they encounter public opposition.

Thus a prison in the United States must always be considered as an institution importantly shaped and continually influenced by the cultural environment in which it operates. A prison not only operates within a given culture, it is, in fact, a part of the culture. The general cultural setting of a prison is important because the individuals who make up the prison staff, as well as the majority of the inmates, are drawn from that setting and have been shaped by it. A prison in a rural location is different from a prison in an urban complex in part because of the environmental differences. As sociologist T. Lynn Smith has pointed out:

> Farm folk differ from urban people, and rural society differs from urban society, principally because of the different environments impinging upon the two populations. Undoubtedly the environmental factors and conditions are the influences that are chiefly responsible for the contrasting patterns of behavior to be found in the two populations; and a knowledge of the fundamental characteristics of the rural situation should contribute much to an understanding of the structure of rural society, the way it functions, the operation of social controls in the rural group, and the manner in which social change proceeds in the rural districts.[1]

The Mississippi State Penitentiary is, first of all, located in a rural environment. Mississippians are, and always have been, primarily a rural people. Although the percentage of people living in urban areas in Mississippi has been increasing, especially since 1950, the rate has been slow. The Census of 1960 showed that only 37.7 percent of all Mississippians lived in urban areas. Prior to 1950, less than 20 percent of the people in the state lived in the city. There seems little doubt that Mississippi's predominantly rural character is a variable influencing its penal institution and any other establishment in the state.

While one may not make a simple dichotomy of rural and urban communities, the differences between rural and urban modes of living may be considered to be the

[1] T. Lynn Smith, *The Sociology of Rural Life* (New York, 1953), 15.

product of such closely integrated and functionally related attributes as: occupation, size of community, density of population, physical environment, social differentiation, and social interaction. All of these factors have more or less been an influence upon the circumstances in which conjugal visiting developed at Parchman. They also give the rural family, the most intimately involved institution in conjugal visiting, its distinctiveness.

Of all the factors mentioned above, occupational difference is of the most fundamental importance. Agriculture and the various forms of agricultural enterprises are the basis of the rural economy. Although rural people may work at many different occupations, the nature of agriculture as an occupation gives rural life its flavor. A distinguishing characteristic of most farming is that it is a family undertaking; the farmer nearly always lives in the midst of his occupation and typically shares it with other members of his family. The farmer lives his life among neighbors who are also farmers. The sameness of activity is socially important because it gives to the rural community a homogeneity of interests characteristic of few other groups.

The conditions surrounding the agricultural mode of earning a living give rise in turn to other characteristics of rural life. The nature of farming demands a large area of land per person. Even the most intensive agricultural systems do not approach the density of a city. In 1960, for example, the United States as a whole had a population density of 50.5 persons per square mile. At the same time, the density of population in the rural United States was 19 persons per square mile; in the rural-farm population characteristic of Mississippi, there were approximately 8 persons per square mile.[2] These differences are important in giving the general cast to many aspects of rural life. Low density of population is favorable to intimate social relationships and to other forms of social interaction possible only in small primary groups. Although low density of population may mean a scarcity of social contacts, the quality of these contacts is enhanced because they are composed largely of direct face-to-face relations. The social contacts of the rural person are not only intimate and personal but also tend to be of a lasting nature.

As a result of the factors mentioned above, there is a basic difference in the social solidarity or social cohesion of rural and urban communities. The rural world is characterized by a social unity based on similarities in traits and objectives and sameness of experience.[3] Rural solidarity is based upon informal, personal, and noncontractual relationships. The majority of administrative officials, staff members, and inmates of the Mississippi State Penitentiary are individuals who grew up in a rural pattern of interaction. Therefore, the staff at Parchman is used to less superficial, less standardized, and more personal contacts with the inmates than staff members of prisons in urban environments who are more accustomed to dealing with all individuals categorically.

Since Parchman is a penal plantation actively engaged in

[2] Ralph Thomlinson, *Population Dynamics* (New York, 1965), 521–24.

[3] This distinction is, of course, that made by Emile Durkheim. See George Simpson, *Emile Durkheim on the Division of Labor in Society* (New York, 1933).

large-scale farming, those selected for positions on the staff, and particularly for the important post of camp sergeant, must have had experience as farmers. Thus, even though the total population of Mississippi is rural, the prison staff members are necessarily more rural than the state population as a whole. The camp sergeants must direct the farm work of the inmates in their camps, and therefore, to insure sound agricultural management, it is vital that they be individuals with farm backgrounds. With the exception of a few, such as hospital employees, the staff members of Parchman have lived all their lives as rural people.

That the environmental background of Parchman's officials is a major factor characterizing the rather informal relationships between staff and inmates is especially important to the conjugal visiting program. Because it is a practice disfavored in American society generally and hence rarely discussed or openly advocated in penology conferences and formal meetings, conjugal visiting is better suited to the informal situation of Parchman than to the formal, contractual relationships found in many other American prisons. In an institution where informality prevails, new developments may occur without one having to go through the "chain of command" and the bureaucratic process. Therefore, when viewed as a practice more likely to develop in an informal, noncontractual institution, conjugal visiting seems not less likely but more likely to have developed in the Mississippi State Penitentiary than anywhere else in the United States.

The influence of the rural environment upon marital and family relationships should also be noted since they have a direct relationship to conjugal visiting. The stability of the rural family is a widely accepted fact.[4] As a union of husband and wife, parents and children, the rural family is much more closely integrated and more permanent than the urban family as divorce statistics show.[5] And in comparison with other social institutions, the role of the family is considered to be much more important in the country than in the city. Although little study has been made of the sexual adjustment of husband and wife in the farm setting, the entire environment of the farm family suggests the "normality" of sex, reproduction, and other life processes. While it is doubtful that the "naturalness" of sex in the rural situation is an important factor in making conjugal visiting acceptable, the stability and high regard with which the family is held in rural Mississippi were probably important factors in the initiation of the practice at Parchman. A prison in a rural culture where both staff and inmates have high regard for the stability of marriage can be expected to make efforts to safeguard a marriage even though the husband is imprisoned. As has been noted, the Mississippi penitentiary, besides allowing wives to visit their husbands, also allows all members of the family to visit in a group and individually.

It has also been mentioned that Parchman has an inmate furlough program which allows inmates to visit their homes for other than reasons of emergency. (This latter

[4] A good discussion of the rural family and its solidarity and cohesion may be seen in John H. Kolb and Edmund Des Brunner, *A Study of Rural Society* (Boston, 1952), Chap. 11.

[5] Paul H. Landis, *Rural Life in Progress* (New York, 1948), 319.

privilege applies to single inmates as well as to married prisoners.) The rural culture of Mississippi not only emphasizes the marital relationship but also the stability of the entire family as well. Therefore, conjugal visiting in Mississippi is, in part, a manifestation of the rural emphasis on stable families.[6]

The high regard in which Mississippians hold the family has also been important in making the conjugal visiting practice acceptable to the officials of the state as well as to the public. Local newspapers have carried stories of the "family visits" at the penitentiary without mustering public opposition to the program. The fact that conjugal visiting is believed to help in keeping marriages and families from breaking up makes the people of the state not only accept the practice but take pride in it as well.

The fact that the penitentiary is actually a plantation also has a bearing on conjugal visiting. While it might seem enough to point out that the penitentiary is a farming institution in a rural environment with basic rural-agricultural influences, it is necessary to recognize the influences associated with the plantation system itself for there are important variations within the agricultural occupation. Although there are not as many skills, techniques, specializations, and differences in agricultural enterprises as compared with urban occupations, specialization does take place; and with the specializations, there are different

---

[6] It is relevant to note, as another indication of "familism" in Mississippi, the "sleeping-in" hospital. In many Mississippi hospitals, when a person is admitted as a patient, the hospital allows his family to stay overnight with him, providing beds for them as well as for the patient.

rhythms of daily, weekly, monthly, and seasonal activities. Each type of farming, in short, interposes a different pattern of life. Cotton farming is not the same as farming in the corn belt, and both are different from tobacco farming or fruit growing. Not only differing rhythms of life accompany each type of farming, but the amount and nature of the rewards derived from the various types of farming also cause differences among farmers.

The plantation system is one of the most distinctive types of farming. Moreover, a cotton plantation is different in many respects from other types of plantations.[7] The plantation on which the Mississippi State Penitentiary is located falls into an organizational pattern of farming having social implications and consequences associated with no other type of agriculture. A large cotton plantation, more than any other kind of plantation, has the character of being a community in itself,[8] and it has the tendency to develop its own particular patterns of interaction.

Since the plantation is a system which tends to perpetuate itself, the essential patterns of interaction in the system remain, even though formal relationships between the participants may be altered. On the plantations of the South that withstood the Civil War, the sharecropper or tenant farmer system displaced the old slave system. For a satisfactory share of the crops, landlords agreed to "furnish" their tenants with the necessities of life until

[7] Smith, *The Sociology of Rural Life,* Chap. 14. See also Morton Rubin, *Plantation County* (Chapel Hill, 1951).

[8] Charles P. Loomis and J. Allen Beegle, *Rural Sociology* (Englewood Cliffs, 1957), 155.

harvesttime. Although the cropper system was technically different from the slave system, the cropper's independence was only nominal and the relationships between the cropper and the planter were simply variations of the slave and master theme. Whatever the nominal relationships among the individuals who operate a plantation, the elements of the system remain and set the character of the personal interaction. The essential features in the plantation way of life always include concentration of landownership, centralized control of a large force of workers, and specialization by tasks. These aspects of the plantation system remain at Parchman even though it is a penal institution. And since the Mississippi State Penitentiary is built upon the plantation structure and performs the basic functions of a plantation, it cannot escape, at a general level, evidencing the essential patterns of interaction characteristic of the plantation system.

An important concomitant of the plantation system has been found to be the social process of accommodation.[9] While accommodation is a term having several usages, it is, above all, a reciprocal adjustment between two or more parties to conflict. Accommodation also applies to adjustment which prevents or minimizes conflict. It may occur without conscious awareness, particularly on the level of interpersonal relations.

The plantation organization is dependent upon an accommodative relationship between the landlord and the laborer, whether he is a slave, sharecropper, cash tenant, or even a prisoner. A study sponsored by the Federal Emer-

[9] Smith, *The Sociology of Rural Life,* 318.

gency Relief Administration, inquiring into the nature of the accommodative processes on plantations, found that the conventional attitude on any type of plantation is a paternalistic one.[10] The landlord must in any case satisfy, in some fashion, the basic needs of the workers. It is essential to the successful operation of a plantation.

While all prisons afford some form of accommodation in their functioning, the penal plantation system especially favors the accommodative process. It is an organizational form in which the accommodation process is endemic; it is a system in which basic needs of workers must be met if the system is to be maintained. Consequently, the penal plantation may be viewed as a prison adaptation in which the sexual needs of the inmates will be given more consideration. It provides a general setting which favors concession on the part of the institutional officials and staff.

In addition to being a self-contained sociocultural system in which accommodation is always present, the plantation is fundamentally a business enterprise. It is an economic institution operated for profit by an owner and his assistants. Parchman, as a plantation prison, is also such an institution. It has an economic base in which the goal is high and efficient production on the part of the individual worker. Therefore, Parchman can be expected to be more adaptive to the needs of the worker. And sex, being such a basic and persistent need among young males, is, of course, a factor to be taken into consideration when economic goals are given a place of prominence. That the

[10] Harold C. Hoffsomer, *Landlord-Tenant Relation and Relief in Alabama* (Washington, 1935).

Mississippi State Penitentiary has always emphasized the economic becomes a not incidental factor in the development of the conjugal visit.

The economic factor was more important in the origin of the conjugal visit at Parchman, however, than in the present-day operation of the practice. The economics of the penitentiary and its compatibility with conjugal visiting does not rule out the more constructive aspects of the practice and other motivations behind the granting of the privilege. As the program has developed over the years, the attitudes of the staff members have progressed to a point where they have moved beyond an accommodative relationship. The economic base of the penal plantation, quite strong in earlier days, is merely a general aspect of the system which favored the development of conjugal visits, and it represents part of the accommodative pattern inherent in the plantation as a functioning institution.

The small size of the camps at Parchman is a very important aspect of the penitentiary amenable to the successful functioning of its conjugal visiting program.[11] The inmates are housed in small, self-contained camps with each camp somewhat isolated from the others. Camp Ten, the largest in the penitentiary, has fewer than two hundred inmates. Seven of the camps for men have fewer than a hundred inmates, and three have fewer than fifty. The small camps have several characteristics which favored the

[11] The use of the word "successful" does not necessarily imply that the program is beneficial in rehabilitation of the prisoners, although it may be. It is, rather, used to mean that the program has operated with little friction or problems.

development of conjugal visiting, and which are vital to its continued operation.

The small, semi-isolated camp structure was favorable to the development of conjugal visiting in part because it simply increased the probability of its development. Since the camps are separated from each other by a distance of two miles, on the average, there was no opportunity for systematic and frequent communication among the camps when the program first started.[12] The camps followed the same time schedules in their daily routines, but each camp developed variations in meeting specific problems. Each camp was, and at present still is, under the direct authority and supervision of a sergeant who in his responsibilities is analogous to the captain of a military company. Although he has standing orders and regulations which he must follow and enforce, and almost daily receives special orders, there are many occasions when he has the freedom to form policy within his camp.

In the case of visiting privileges at Parchman, the penitentiary establishes the days and hours of visitation and specifies the people who may visit inmates. The individual camp sergeant, however, is responsible for searching them and supervising their visits within the camps. Under such a program of visitation, with each camp responsible for its own supervision, there is a greater opportunity for conjugal visiting to develop than in an institution where all inmates are housed in one central prison where uniformity is emphasized.

[12] The penitentiary now has telephone and radio communication systems connecting all camps.

The small camps present fewer problems in terms of security, particularly in the reception and supervision of visitors. In a prison where inmates are centrally confined, visiting days usually bring a large number of people who want to visit inmates; in large prisons, the number of people coming to visit will often be two or three hundred or more. Consequently, security precautions and supervision must be strict. In a camp at Parchman housing only a hundred inmates the number of visitors coming on a single day is never large. In the smaller camps, perhaps only ten or fifteen visitors will arrive on a single day. This situation affords greater freedom of visitation generally, and the resulting more informal conditions thus provide the possibilities of conjugal visiting. In terms of couples who wish to use the conjugal visiting facilities, the smaller number results in a more respectable and less embarrassing situation. This precludes, for example, such things as couples standing in line waiting their turn, being rushed in and out of the rooms, and other such occurrences in which embarrassment would be certain. It is much easier to evolve and maintain a working system of interpersonal relations in any activity where numbers are small. In the case of conjugal visiting, small numbers are basic, for sexual relations are of course the most intimate of all human activities.

The small camps also allow the sergeants to get to know their inmates personally. Furthermore, a sergeant gets to know a prisoner's wife and entire family if they visit. The fact that he knows the man's wife is very important for this means less formality in the reception and security

precautions. The wife does not have to establish her iden-
tity after the first few visits. When she appears at the camp
on visiting day, she is greeted by name and security precautions can be held to a minimum. The small camps thus
present the wife with a less rigid and more comfortable
situation than would a large prison. As a result, she is able
to relax and is not constantly reminded of the prison setting. Such an atmosphere allows wives to keep their self-
respect and to feel that the visit has indeed been a private
one. The informal, personal treatment of wives is emphasized by all of the camp sergeants. They stress, furthermore, that the wives be treated with respect and courtesy, a
practice which they feel is tremendously important.

While no active counseling is given to prisoners whose
wives visit them, the fact that the sergeants know the men
well does lead to some effort to help individual inmates.
Several of the sergeants interviewed said that when they
noticed an inmate's morale had been affected by his wife's
failure to visit him, they would contact her and tell her
that they felt her husband needed to see her. Two sergeants mentioned that at least on one occasion they had
bought an inmate's wife a bus ticket to Parchman when
she was not otherwise able to come. The efforts of the
sergeants in this regard reflect the genuine concern which
they develop for inmates in their personal interaction with
them.

The area around each camp is big enough so that inmates and their visitors may enjoy privacy. They may also
walk around the grounds of the camp unguarded. A couple
walking to the conjugal visiting facility doesn't appear con-

spicuous, for several couples may be walking from one area to another at any given moment. While such a feature as the inconspicuousness of the visits may seem trivial, the mores regulating sexual behavior in the United States make this aspect important. It reduces the "obviousness" of the visits objected to by many penologists who do not favor conjugal visiting.

The small camps at Parchman, therefore, are of fundamental importance to the conjugal visiting program. They provide a setting in which relaxed security precautions enable inmates and their visitors freedom to visit without close supervision. It should also be mentioned that the small camps allow feelings of identification and cooperation on the part of inmates, particularly single inmates who do not have the privilege. The program could hardly function in a setting of obscenity, jokes, or disrespect for wives. As it operates at Parchman, single inmates sometimes even care for the children of an inmate and his wife while the couple are in the red house. Such occurrences reveal (and indeed depend upon) a spirit of cooperation characteristic of a social unit in which primary relationships predominate. It is a condition difficult to achieve when numbers are large.

There can be little doubt of the significance of racial segregation in the initiation of conjugal visits at Parchman. The practice began in the Negro camps where the white staff members were tolerant of the inmates' sexual needs. Although the Negroes' position as members of the "lower caste" had its disadvantages, it did relieve them of the moral restraints which the white society imposed on all whites, including white prisoners. At the time Parchman was established, Negroes were typically viewed by white southerners as being "naturally" promiscuous and as having greater sexual needs. The white sergeants of Negro camps simply "looked the other way" in accommodating what they considered to be natural among Negroes. As the buildings used for conjugal visiting appeared in Negro camps and as the practice became more respectable, it was accepted in the white camps.

At the present time, segregation of the camps at Parchman precludes conflict of the races in the most carefully guarded aspect of their interaction—that of sexual behavior. It is quite likely that enforced racial integration of the camps would be followed immediately by the termination of the conjugal visiting privilege. The existing taboos governing the relationships between the two races are so strong that conjugal visiting in its present form would be almost impossible in Mississippi in the absence of segregated camps.[13]

Conjugal visiting at Parchman appears to be the product of a social organization built upon several crucial factors: rurality, plantation social system, economic motivation, small camp structure, and segregation of the races. When one looks at conjugal visiting and this network of organization, it no longer seems paradoxical that the practice developed at the Mississippi State Penitentiary instead of at a prison in another setting. The conjugal visit at Parch-

[13] For a discussion of the nature and severity of Negro-white sexual taboos, see Raymond W. Mack, *Race, Class and Power* (New York, 1968), Chap. 3.

man is not a product of formal intentions or planning; it is, rather, a product of the nature of the penitentiary and the character of the relationships which that nature engenders. It may be looked upon as a latent function of the social organization and a consequence of accommodative relationships inherent in the plantation as a social system.

The question of why conjugal visiting developed in Mississippi can, of course, never be settled with certainty. The argument presented here has not been that the structure and organization of the Mississippi State Penitentiary *caused* its development, but that it *allowed* the practice to develop. Conjugal visiting does not always emerge out of such a system. Other state prisons in the United States have several characteristics of Parchman. Both Arkansas and Louisiana, for example, have penal plantation systems. In the institutions of these states, however, prisoners have not been housed in as many camps as have those in Mississippi. In addition, Mississippi has retained fewer inmates per camp. In no other penal system in the United States have all five of the factors discussed come together with the intensity that exists in the Mississippi penitentiary. The difference is not one of kind but one of degree. Mississippi has not been simply a rural state, but the most rural of all states. The difference in degree is true also in regard to the penal plantation system. While other states have used penal farms, no other has built its penal system in the classic pattern of a large cotton plantation. Throughout most of its history, Parchman has been operated like any other large Delta plantation in which economic motivation was dominant. Few prisons would aspire for the title of being the "most informal." What informality means, simply stated, is that few rules exist and those which do are not followed closely. Plantation accommodation, of which Parchman has given evidence, boils down to a matter of "You help me and I'll help you." In an institution with accommodation and informality prevailing, one can expect unusual developments and concession to inmate needs.

The fact that the conjugal visiting program developed in an unofficial, unplanned manner does not, however, necessarily mean that it is undesirable. It merely indicates the magnitude of the problem of sexual adjustment in prisons. It is to be expected that penal institutions will, when the relationships between the inmates and staff become accommodative or cooperative, whatever the motivation, turn attention to the sexual problems of inmates. Nor should the fact that conjugal visiting developed informally through accommodation rather than from the correctional philosophies of the staff members of the Mississippi State Penitentiary be taken to mean that they do not support the program in an enthusiastic manner. By their expressions it is evident that they do. In fact, most would agree with a veteran camp sergeant who said to the writer in 1963: "I don't know of anything that's more important. It's a touching sight to see a man and his wife greet each other on visiting day. I'd hate to have to tell my men that conjugal visiting was going to stop. Not only because of the fuss it might cause but because I believe it's the right thing to do. You just look at the faces of these men on visiting day and you can see it."

It is also likely that prison administrators and staff members elsewhere would like to do something about the problem of sexual adjustment in their prisons. The structure and organization of Parchman have allowed the staff members to attempt to do something about it through the conjugal visiting program which evolved there.

Chapter IV

Evaluations and Attitudes

Is the conjugal visiting program at Parchman a success? Do the prisoners themselves feel that it is a success? Do the staff members feel that it is a success? And if it has succeeded, in what ways has it succeeded? Is there evidence, for instance, that it has helped to reduce the problem of homosexuality which plagues all prisons; or that it has had the effect of making the inmates more cooperative? Do the single inmates resent the married men having this privilege? How do the wives of inmates feel about the program?

In seeking the answers to these and other questions, two methods were employed. One was to interview camp sergeants, prisoners, wives of prisoners, and former prisoners and their wives. The second method involved the use of a questionnaire which was answered by prisoners using the conjugal visiting privilege as well as by those not using it. The questionnaire and comparative analyses drawn from it will be discussed further in the following chapter.

The most important question concerning a program of conjugal visiting is whether it helps to reduce the problem of homosexuality in prison. Although sexual problems in prisons are admittedly great, criminologists and penologists have been reluctant to give much attention to them. Those who have studied sexual problems in American prisons, however, have not painted a pretty picture. A man familiar with prisons has written: "The most difficult problem a warden faces is homosexuality. Homosexuality causes more quarrels, fights, knifings, and punishment in prison than any other single problem." [1]

Estimates of the extent of homosexuality in prison vary. Some who have studied penal institutions contend that as many as 95 percent of the inmates are involved in homosexual experiences at some time or other during their sentences.[2] Although only a small number of researchers think the rate of homosexuality is that high, almost all would agree that half of the inmates in the average prison are involved in homosexual relationships. The authors of a recent book, *Problems of Homosexuality in Corrections,* point out that "so long as healthy men and women are segregated according to sex, there will remain a fertile field for homosexual tendencies. Even the best wardens in the best prisons cannot cope with this problem . . . . *It cannot be eliminated in such an unwholesome environment.*" [3] One of the reasons the incidence of homosexuality is so high in prison is that not all inmates involved in it are participating by choice. The most objectionable aspect of prison homosexuality is that many young men are forced to become homosexuals by the older, tougher convicts.

In many prisons the men who engage in homosexuality are called "wolves," "punks," or "fags." [4] The "wolf" or

[1] John Barlow Martin, *Break Down the Walls* (New York, 1954), 177.

[2] *Ibid.,* 178. See also Joseph Fishman, *Sex in Prison* (New York, 1934).

[3] Clyde B. Vedder and Patricia G. King, *Problems of Homosexuality in Corrections* (Springfield, Ill., 1967), 25.

[4] Gresham M. Sykes, *The Society of Captives* (New York, 1966). 95.

"jocker" is an aggressive homosexual who attempts to make conquests. He is usually masculine in appearance and older than the average prisoner. His primary object is the "punk," a young prisoner who is forced to submit to a homosexual relationship if he cannot be seduced. The "fag" is a homosexual who plays the female role. Fags become the prison "girls," and try to appear as feminine as possible. They are usually homosexual before coming to prison, leading prisoners to say that "Punks are made but fags are born." Fags are generally given female nicknames, and many prisoners come to look upon them as women. Since the fag does not suffer sexual deprivation in prison, he may very well be happier there than in the free world.

Recent studies of sexual problems in the Philadelphia prison system led the investigators to say that sexual assaults were epidemic in the prisons of that city. From a sample of 5 percent of the inmates who passed through the Philadelphia prison system between June 1, 1966, and July 31, 1968, a total of 156 cases of sexual assaults were documented. Taking into consideration the small sample and the reluctance of the prisoners to disclose sexual assaults, it was estimated that some 2,000 sexual assaults involving 1,500 individual victims and 3,500 individual aggressors occurred during the two-year period.[5] The investigators concluded that virtually every slightly built young man committed by the courts is sexually approached within hours after his admission to prison.

Often young prisoners are overwhelmed and "raped" by gangs of older inmates. Only the tougher and more

[5] *Report on Sexual Assaults in the Philadelphia Prison System,* 3.

hardened young men in prison escape sexual abuse. After a young inmate has been assaulted, he is a "punk" and is marked as a sexual victim for the rest of his confinement. One young prisoner in Philadelphia related his experience as follows:

> I was laying in my bed when seven or eight inmates came to my bed, pulled the blanket off me, put it on the floor and told me to pull my pants down and lay face down on the blanket. I said "no" and was punched in the face by one of the inmates. The inmate that punched me stated if I did not get on the floor the other inmates would gang up on me.

> I got on the floor and my pants and shorts were pulled off. Two inmates spread and held my legs apart while two more inmates held my hands in front of me. While I was being buggered from behind another inmate would make me suck his penis. This continued until all the inmates had attacked me and I heard one of them say it was 1:30 a.m. so let's go to bed. They put me on the bed, covered me with the blanket and one of them patted me on the behind saying "good boy we will see you again tomorrow night." [6]

Homosexual favors in prison are also purchased with luxuries such as cigarettes, candy, or extra food pilfered from the kitchen. In some instances male prostitutes are created by a combination of bribery and persuasion as well as by the threat of force. Typically, an inexperienced young inmate will be "given" cigarettes, candy, or other items by a more experienced prisoner who, after a few

[6] *Ibid.*, 1.

days, will demand sexual favors as repayment. If the young inmate submits, he is branded as a punk and he is pressed into prostitution for the remainder of his imprisonment.

From the psychological point of view, there are three levels of sexual adjustment in prisons: so-called normal, quasi-abnormal, and abnormal.[7] Normal sexual adjustment consists basically of masturbation and sublimation of sexual impulses through work, exercise, or reading. The length of time a man will remain in normal adjustment, however, is not certain, and an inmate who is in a normal level may, as time goes on, come to behave in a quasi-abnormal way, and eventually sink to an abnormal level.

Quasi-abnormal sexual adjustment is technically homosexual behavior, but it is engaged in merely as a substitute for heterosexual activity. Such an inmate's sexual motivation is still toward females and his self-concept remains that of a male. An inmate's behavior stays in the quasi-abnormal category until his homosexuality becomes an end in itself and is no longer looked upon as a substitute for heterosexual relationships. The inmates in the abnormal category, therefore, are definitely habituated to homosexual practice.

The craving which can lead a man into homosexual experiences in prison has been described by an inmate as follows:

To the man dying of hunger and thirst it makes little difference that the only available food and water are tainted. Likewise it makes little or no difference to the average

[7] Donald Clemmer, *The Prison Community* (New York, 1958), Chap. 10.

The conjugal visits allow a prisoner to retain a strong identification with his wife. And since he has this right, he is able to keep the self-image of a man who is still important to others.

The buildings to which married prisoners take their wives are known as "red houses." Most of the buildings were constructed out of whatever scrap lumber and other materials the inmates and the sergeant could secure.

In the First Offenders Camp, the "red house" (right) was included in the camp plan from the beginning, and it is made of the same brick and other materials as the main building itself. The building to the left is the chapel.

Surrounded by a high fence, including a guard tower, Maximum Security is entered through electrically controlled gates. The unit contains cells for inmates convicted of capital crimes and sentenced to death.

It is possible to drive through on the highway without seeing signs to distinguish Parchman from any other large plantation in the area. The penitentiary buildings are similar to those of any other large cotton plantation.

Although visiting hours do not begin until one o'clock every other Sunday afternoon, the visitors begin arriving at any time after midmorning.

"I can't tell you how much it meant to me to be able to be with my wife. You can't understand it without being in the penitentiary."

"I like to see other people's families—children, women. It beats looking at the same faces all the time. I don't think any inmate objects to the visitors anybody has. When you have to stay here all the time, man, you just like to look at new faces no matter who they are visiting."

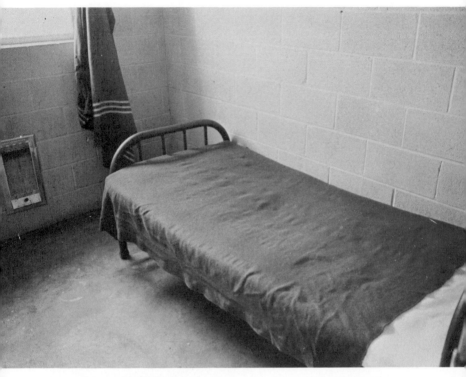

Rooms in the "red house" at the First Offenders Camp afford privacy equal to the rooms in a modern motel, though they are by comparison rather spartan.

prisoner that his only available means of sexual satisfaction are abnormal. It is merely a matter of satisfying as best he can the hunger that besets him. I mean the hunger not only for sexual intercourse but the hunger for the voice, the touch, the laugh, the tears of woman; a hunger for woman herself.[8]

In attempting to obtain the most meaningful evaluations of the influence of conjugal visiting by the institutional staff at Parchman, attention was directed to the camp sergeants, the individuals who have the most contact with the inmate population. The sergeant lives a very short distance from the camp building and is in fact on duty twenty-four hours a day. The average sergeant spends at least twelve hours a day with his inmates. He knows each of his charges well and he comes to know the members of their families who visit the penitentiary.

It is the sergeant's duty to censor the mail of each of the inmates in his camp—the letters which he writes as well as those which he receives. All disturbances and problems among his inmates come to the sergeant's attention, and are usually settled by him. If an inmate has a problem, he takes it to his sergeant. Furthermore, when a member of a prisoner's family comes to the penitentiary with a problem, he is referred first to the camp sergeant. Consequently, the camp sergeants come to know the inmates much more thoroughly than do the other staff members. In the case of conjugal visiting as it operates at Parchman, the camp sergeants are the only employees who know which inmates do and do not have the visits. Inquiries dealing with staff

[8] Victor Nelson, *Prison Days and Nights* (Boston, 1932), 143.

members' evaluations of the influence of the conjugal visiting program were directed, therefore, to the sergeants of
the fourteen camps which have conjugal visiting privileges.

Each sergeant was asked questions relating to the sexual
behavior, discipline, work, and cooperation of his inmates.
Each was also asked what, if any, problems had developed
relating to the conjugal visits and what changes he would
like to see made in the program as it is now being practiced.

The first question directed to the sergeants concerned
the extent of homosexuality in their camps. While it is
obviously impossible for a camp sergeant to have a completely accurate knowledge of the extent of such behavior,
the sergeants were asked on the basis of incidents of it
coming to their attention to rate homosexuality in their
camps as: 1) a very big problem, 2) definitely a problem,
3) a small problem, or 4) a very small problem. Only one
of the fourteen rated homosexuality a very big problem;
six considered it definitely a problem; five said it was a
small problem; and two said they considered it to be only
a very small problem. When examining these responses, it
must be taken into consideration that some of the sergeants
may be more tolerant of the problem of homosexuality in
their camps or may even have different interpretations of
what homosexuality actually is. It is interesting to note
that the problem was considered greater by sergeants in
charge of camps which contained the most prisoners. This
was true for both white and Negro camps. At the time the
sergeants were interviewed, those rating homosexuality as
a "very big problem" or "definitely a problem" had camps

which averaged 136 men; those which rated it as a small problem averaged only 52 men per camp.

The selection of inmates for the various camps is another factor to be considered in the differing reports of homosexuality. Several of the small camps house men who have been chosen because of their good behavior. The sergeant who considered homosexuality a very big problem was in charge of a large camp for white men. "Everybody on the farm knows I've got the worst men in my camp," he said. "Some of the camps are like Sunday school beside mine." When he was asked what percentage of the men in his camp engaged in homosexuality, he answered: "That's not possible to say for sure. Oh, I don't know— right now I know it's bad, more so than ordinary, at least I've been bothered more here lately. If I had to say how many I'd say 25 or 30 percent do it. It might go higher than that but not lower. Let's just put it between 25 and 50 percent. I know that would cover it."

The homosexuality discussed by the sergeants appeared to cover the range found in other prisons, but there was little mention of younger inmates being attacked by the older prisoners. Usually the sergeants spoke of "sissies" who willingly engaged in homosexual relations, both orally and anally. A sergeant who rated his Negro camp as having a big problem with homosexuality said:

> You wouldn't believe some of the things that happen. These guys fall in love with each other. Some of these sissies act just like high school girls, prissing around, plucking eyebrows. They go steady and get married. Hell, it wouldn't surprise me if one got pregnant. That's most of it, these

sissies. Some of them are Lulus. You can't put a stop to it, at least we never have been able to. Most of them come here that way. You can't put a stop to it here if he does it in the free world. Just about every fight you have, you can bet some sissy is mixed up in it somewhere.

The sergeants who rated homosexuality a small problem seemed confident in their estimations. They felt that their men were better behaved in most respects than those in some of the large farm camps. A sergeant in charge of one of the units with the fewest men spoke with pride about his camp: "I'm not going to say I don't have any problems with these men because you'd know I was lying, and I do have problems, any man does. But I never have to worry about homosexuals here, at least not so far. I've got a lot of respect for my men. They work hard, do good work. I'd put them up against any crew you could find. Give me the lowest rate you got there. It's a very small problem here."

When asked to compare homosexual activity among inmates who had conjugal visits with that among those who did not, eleven of the sergeants said inmates receiving conjugal visits engaged in much less homosexuality. The remaining three rated inmates receiving conjugal visits as engaging in a little less. All believed, however, that, as a group, those receiving conjugal visits engaged in less homosexuality. Most of those who said men participating in the conjugal visiting program engaged in much less homosexuality were sergeants in charge of the largest camps. Although they rated their camps as having a big problem with homosexuality, they said those receiving conjugal visits had much less to do with it. The man quoted earlier who considered homosexuality a very big problem in his camp said:

> Yes sir, I can tell a difference. The men that get visits from their wives don't get mixed up in it much at all. I wish all of them had wives. You see, the ones that give you the most trouble are them that have forgotten what women are like. They are no good, to themself or anybody else. To tell you the truth, they are just about crazy. They wouldn't use conjugal visits if they could. They honestly had rather be with a man than a woman. That's the ones you have to look out for. They never even think of women. They think a boy looks better than a real woman. That's what makes me mad—when some freak tries to bust a young boy. I won't put up with that.

A man who had been employed for four years in another southern prison before accepting a job at Parchman responded to the question as follows:

> A man would be a fool if he said he knew everything that went on in his camp, but I'll tell you this: Anybody that works in a prison has a pretty good idea how much homosexual stuff there is. It's bad here, but the problem in this camp is nothing compared to what I knew about in the other prison where I worked. In that place, I'd have to say it was the biggest problem we had. Just about every day a fight or some other disturbance took place. I know conjugal visits help. I've never had a single case that I remember when the man's wife is visiting him. It don't cure the problem—you can't expect it to—but it does help it some. You can't tell me any different. It will help keep a man straight.

The sergeants were reluctant to speak of the problem of homosexuality in terms of the percentage of inmates involved in it. No sergeant, however, believed more than 50 percent of his men participated in it. Judging from the statements of the sergeants, therefore, the rate of homosexuality in the small camps appears lower than the rate of about 50 percent in most prisons. In the larger camps, however, the sergeants' statements describing the extent of homosexuality do not differ greatly from the situation in other institutions.

The homosexual terminology employed at other prisons is also widely understood at Parchman, but not consistently used from camp to camp. The terms "wolf," "jocker," and "top-men" are recognized by staff and inmates as describing aggressive homosexuals. There is also a distinction between "punks" and "fags," although these terms are not generally used. A homosexual who voluntarily plays a passive or feminine role is most frequently called a "sissy" at Parchman. If a young prisoner is forced into a homosexual relationship, he may be known as a "gal-boy," "kid," "punk kid," or simply "boy."

In comparing disciplinary problems of inmates using the conjugal visiting and those who do not, six sergeants reported that they could tell no difference in this regard. Four sergeants, however, said that those receiving conjugal visits gave them much less trouble and four said they gave a little less trouble. When asked to compare the inmates' willingness to work, five did not hesitate to say that those receiving conjugal visits were much better in this respect. An additional five said those receiving conjugal visits were somewhat better workers. Four sergeants of small units, however, said they could tell no difference. One sergeant of a Negro camp, reflecting an attitude more typical of an earlier era at Parchman, believed conjugal visits greatly improved the work of his inmates. Of the men receiving conjugal visits, he said: "Oh yeah, they are better workers. If you let a nigger have some on Sunday, he will really go out and do some work for you on Monday."

When asked about the over-all cooperation of those receiving conjugal visits as compared to other inmates, three of the sergeants said that those receiving conjugal visits were a little more cooperative. Eleven were convinced that those having conjugal visits were much more cooperative.

The sergeants were also asked what they believed to be the most helpful aspect of the conjugal visiting program at Parchman. One sergeant said the work of the inmates was most importantly influenced in his judgment; four felt that the visits were most helpful in producing cooperative attitudes among inmates; two others suggested the reduction of homosexual behavior. Seven of the fourteen sergeants, however, said they believed the most helpful aspect and the chief purpose of the visits was to keep marriages from breaking up.

Twelve camp sergeants did not feel that the program caused any extra work for them. They said, rather, that they had to be on the job all of the time anyway. One sergeant believed that the practice actually saved him work in some instances. The freedom of visiting privileges in general, he said, kept the prisoner's wife and other family members from worrying so much and making inquiries about him. When an inmate and his wife can see each other in private, talk freely, and even have intercourse, he said, they do not often have to come to him for help or information. Speaking of this facet of conjugal visiting he said:

> Most problems the inmates have are concerned with worry about their families. And most people who come to the penitentiary are concerned about how the inmate is getting along, how his health is, and so on. The best thing I can do is to allow them to see each other and judge for themselves. A common thing in prison is for a man to worry about his wife, whether or not she still loves him and is faithful to him. One visit in private with him is better than a hundred letters because he can judge for himself.

Two sergeants of Negro camps, however, said that the program caused them extra work in ascertaining whether a woman was the wife of a prisoner. Since some of the Negro prisoners have common-law marriages, which the penitentiary officials wish to respect, the sergeant has to question the female visitors and try to determine whether the visitor and the inmate have actually been living as a married couple. Often, one said, he had to check with people in the prisoner's home community to get more concrete proof of marriage.

As reported by the sergeants who administer it, the conjugal visiting program at Parchman has been operating with a minimum of problems. Only two sergeants mentioned any problems in connection with the program. One sergeant of a Negro camp who had been employed eight years at the penitentiary replied that on one occasion a prostitute had slipped by his screening and had infected an inmate with a venereal disease. Another sergeant of a Negro camp reported that several wives of prisoners had become pregnant. He did not say that the fact that the wives became pregnant had caused any trouble at the penitentiary, but merely cited this as something he felt was a problem associated with conjugal visiting.[9]

Each of the camp sergeants at Parchman said that the facilities provided for the visits should be improved. Even with neglected facilities, all sergeants enthusiastically supported the program as being of basic importance to their camps. Each believed that the program, in general, should be continued as it is being practiced. The changes they felt would be desirable related to the adequacy of the buildings concerned. The sergeants uniformly felt that they needed larger and more attractive red houses which would afford more privacy and a more pleasant atmosphere. Except for the two sergeants who complained of the work in screening wives, the sergeants felt that the informal administration of the program should be continued, since any basic change in administration would curtail the freedom and informality of the visits. They believed these fac-

[9] Although there is no way to tell exactly how many children have been born as a result of the conjugal visiting program at Parchman, the number is not likely to be large. State welfare officials do not consider the practice to be a problem as far as dependent children are concerned. Since Mississippi's welfare program is one of the most strictly regulated in the United States, a prison program which added a significant burden to welfare expenses would probably not be tolerated.

tors to be the most important aspects of the program's success.

A frequently encountered question concerning the functioning of the conjugal visiting program at Parchman is: How do single inmates feel about the married men having the conjugal visiting privilege while they themselves do not? Since the privilege applies only to the married men, it is a categorical privilege which less than half of the total inmate population enjoys. It might be, for example, that the unmarried men in the institution feel the penitentiary is unfair in its treatment of prisoners. If this were the case, then one would expect that a program of conjugal visiting would, as some writers suggest, cause more tension and conflict in the penitentiary than it would reduce.[10]

To obtain an indication of this, one item in the inmate questionnaire was directed to unmarried inmates. The question was stated as follows: "If you are unmarried, do you resent married inmates having the conjugal visiting privilege?" The possible answers were: 1) yes, very much; 2) yes, a little; 3) and no. The great majority of unmarried inmates did not indicate that they resented the privilege being granted to married men. Of 822 who responded to the question, 737 (or 89.6 percent) said they felt no resentment. A total of 85 single men did report some resentment, however. Of that number, 58 (or approximately 7 percent) answered "Yes, very much."

The fact that very nearly nine out of every ten unmarried inmates did not indicate a feeling of resentment over conjugal visits for married men suggests that, for most

[10] Tappan, *Crime, Justice and Correction*, 680.

single inmates, a pattern of relative deprivation operates within the institution in regards to conjugal visits.[11] Unmarried prisoners in the main apparently identify with other unmarried inmates and view the married prisoner and his wife very nearly in the same way unmarried individuals do in a free community. Of several unmarried inmates interviewed by the researcher over the years, only one expressed resentment over married men having the privilege. This prisoner, a man of twenty-six, seemed bitter and hostile toward every aspect of the penitentiary and did not single out the conjugal visiting program especially.

Most prisoners accept the fact that a man and his wife have rights and privileges which do not apply to unmarried men. Just as single men in the general population accept higher rates of taxes and more responsibility in military obligations, so apparently do prison inmates accept the fact that married men have wives who may visit them. A young man, nineteen years of age expressed his views on the matter as follows: "Do I resent married men having conjugal visits? No, I'm not married. Why should I care? That's between him and his wife. I don't see any difference in here and on the outside. If one guy has a mother, say, and she visits him why should a guy who doesn't have a mother resent the guy who does have one? It's the same thing as far as I'm concerned. I'm all for a man and his wife getting together."

Another single man, whose parents were divorced when

[11] See Samuel Stouffer, and others, *The American Soldier* (Princeton, 1958) , Chap. 2.

he was fourteen years old, was very much in favor of conjugal visits. Of the visits he said:

> I approve of conjugal visits between families when the husband is in prison. I've spent a total of seven years in several different institutions and only one of these allows conjugal visits. In Parchman here, I've seen less rioting, less homosexuality, and an altogether different attitude in the inmates in general. I've also seen many families stay together here which I sincerely believe would have been broken in any other institution. I say this because these visits let them have a normal and healthy married life on visiting days, and many problems were solved during the visits that would have resulted in arguments and hard feelings where these visits aren't allowed.

A divorced inmate with a college degree, who was forty years old, spoke of his and other inmates' reactions to the program:

> I've never heard any discussion on the subject whatsoever. I accept it as a normal thing the way it is done here. I can see how resentment could be a problem if the privilege could be bought and sold. The same thing would be true of any privilege. The secret to running a prison or anything, I guess, is being fair in the rules. If some married men weren't allowed the privilege, they would strongly resent it. If my ex-wife and I were still married, I would be very resentful if they didn't allow me to have conjugal visits like the rest of the married men. As it is, I accept the fact that some men have good marriages and I don't. The penitentiary officials have nothing to do with my being divorced.

The most frequent reply encountered in interviews with single prisoners is represented by the response of a young man twenty years old, interviewed in September of 1967. When asked how he felt about married men being able to have conjugal visits he answered: "I like to see other people's families—children, women. It beats looking at the same faces all the time. I don't think any inmate objects to the visitors anybody has. When you have to stay here all the time, man, you just like to look at new faces no matter who they are visiting. It makes it seem less like a prison on visiting days when the free world people come in. Man, I even like to look at their cars."

Since the embarrassment associated with sex in conjugal visits has been considered a negative aspect of the practice, one or two items in the inmate questionnaire were directed toward it. The inmates who received conjugal visits were asked the following question: "If you engage in conjugal visiting, has any other inmate ever acted in any way disrespectful to your wife?" Of 462 inmates answering the question, only 18 (3.9 percent) replied in the affirmative. When asked if the visits were embarrassing to them, 42 (9.1 percent) said they were. When asked if they believed the conjugal visits were embarrassing to their wives, however, 87 (18.8 percent) answered in the affirmative.

The inmates who received conjugal visits were also asked to choose from among several reasons the one for which they believed conjugal visits were most helpful. The reasons from which they had to choose were as follows: keeping marriages from breaking up; reducing homosexuality; making inmates more cooperative; helping rehabilitate in-

mates; making inmates easier to control; and making inmates work harder. Finally, the inmates could indicate
that the visits were helpful for *all* of the above equally.

Of the 464 inmates responding to the question, 234 (or
about half) said they believed that conjugal visits were
most helpful in keeping marriages from breaking up. (As
has been noted earlier, seven of the fourteen camp sergeants also ranked the stability of marriage as the most
important variable in conjugal visiting.) Seventy-five of
the 464 thought reducing homosexuality was the most
helpful aspects of conjugal visits, and 68 replied that they

Table 3

RATING OF THE HELPFULNESS OF CONJUGAL VISITS BY INMATES
RECEIVING CONJUGAL VISITS

For Which of the Following Do You Believe Conjugal Visits to Be Most Helpful?	Number	Percentage
Keeping Marriages From Breaking up	234	50.4
Reducing Homosexuality	75	16.2
Making Inmates More Cooperative	19	4.1
Helping Rehabilitate Inmates	19	4.1
Making Inmates Easier to Control	39	8.4
Making Inmates Work Harder	10	2.2
Helpful for All Equally	68	14.7
Total	464	100.1

were equally important in *all* of the areas. Only 10 inmates
believed conjugal visits were most helpful in making inmates work harder.

The majority of the inmates using the conjugal visiting privilege did not believe that the facilities provided for the visits were satisfactory. When asked to rate the buildings provided for the visits, only 152 of 464, or 32.7 percent, said they considered them satisfactory. Most of the inmates who were interviewed complained that the buildings were too small and that they were in need of repairs.

In an attempt to better evaluate the conjugal visiting program at Parchman, sixteen former inmates and their wives were interviewed. All of the interviews took place in the homes of the couples. In each case, both the man and his wife were interviewed together for about an hour. Then, in order to allow the husband to speak more freely about such things as homosexuality in prison and the reaction of single inmates to conjugal visiting, the wife was excused and the interview continued with the husband alone.

In all of the interviews, the former inmates talked freely about the conjugal visiting program and other phases of life in the penitentiary. Although it was expected that they would talk less favorably about the conjugal visiting program than did inmates still serving sentences, they did not. In fact, in all sixteen cases, the praise of the former inmates was even greater than that of the men still in prison. Since they were not uncritical of other aspects of the penitentiary and did make recommendations which they thought would improve the conjugal visiting program, their high praise of the visits deserves serious consideration.

While most people who hear of conjugal visiting think of sexual release as the only function of the practice, those

who participate in the program speak first of the freedom
of visiting in private with their wives and of being able to
talk intimately and frankly to them without fear of being
heard by the prison authorities. They emphasize the *emotional* satisfaction rather than the *physical* satisfaction. A
man who had been out of prison for more than three years
after serving a sentence for robbery and who appeared to
be, in his words, "over the hill as far as crime is concerned,"
spoke with great appreciation in his voice about the conjugal visiting program.

> It was the only thing I had to look forward to while I was
> in Parchman. Believe me, I never knew how much my wife
> meant to me until I went to prison. She visited me every
> visiting day. She would encourage me and tell me I could
> make it. I was really blue when I first went to Parchman.
> I'll never forget the first time my wife visited me. I cried
> like a baby. But that first visit really helped me. I felt like
> a different man. It was a comfort knowing I could be with
> my wife on visiting day. Truthfully, I don't think I could
> have made it without her help.

His wife also had much praise for the conjugal visiting
program. Of it, she said:

> I think it's pretty wonderful. It helped him and it helped
> me. It made me feel like I was still a wife and not just some-
> thing sitting at home. I never had no desire to go with
> another man, but if I could not have been with J—— I may
> have desired another man. It made me remember that I
> was a married woman. It made J—— appreciate me more.
> The only thing I didn't like was that we had only three
> hours to visit together. Really and truly it brought me and

J—— closer together. We appreciate one another more now. When we were first married we were not too responsible with our money. We would go out and have fun, spend our money before we ever paid our bills or bought our groceries. But now we do these things first. J—— is more responsible now.

A couple who had been married ten years and had three children were interviewed about three months after the husband had been released from Parchman where he had served thirteen months for breaking and entering. Since their home was two hundred miles from the penitentiary, the wife had been able to visit her husband only once a month. Although both spoke favorably of the conjugal visiting program and their experience with it, the wife criticized it as follows:

I wish there was some way to speed up getting into the camp. Sometimes it takes almost an hour to check all of the visitors and their packages in, and then you don't have but two hours left to visit. When you have to travel as far as I did, that waiting to get in to the camp is hard. I also hated to drive back home at night by myself. Everybody at the penitentiary treated me just fine. I'd have to say that the program meant a lot to me. I wish I could have brought the children with me, but I just couldn't take them that far by myself. They only got to see their daddy when he come home on emergency leave when his father died. Also I wish they could change the bed linen for each couple. You know, have linen in the room and let each couple change the bed. That would make it much nicer.

After his wife had left the room, the husband spoke freely about conjugal visiting and homosexuality. While at Parchman, he had been in two camps—one for four months and the other for nine. When asked about how much conjugal visiting influenced homosexual activity in the penitentiary, he said:

> I never did know a man whose wife visited him that ever did any of that stuff. Mostly it was the older cons who had been in prison a long time chasing younger boys. Some of those people just ain't human. There ought to be some way to keep young men in some place by themselves. I've actually seen young men bought and sold by those old cons. I don't honestly believe they're human. It was much worse in the first camp I was in than in the other. I can't tell you how much it meant to me to be able to be with my wife. You can't understand it without being in the penitentiary, but you get to wondering if you yourself could go crazy like them guys. A normal visit with your wife makes you know you're different. I don't see why all prisons don't have these visits. It don't cost nothing. Why, if it saved one man in fifty years it would be worth it.

The first camp he had been in was a large farm camp. He estimated that as many as 25 percent of the inmates there engaged in homosexual activity. He went on to say that he was literally afraid to go to sleep. He said he was not so much afraid of being molested sexually as of being killed or injured. In the second camp, a small unit which housed selected men, he said he never worried. "It was as different as night and day," he stated. "It was like two different prisons."

Fourteen of the couples interviewed were critical of the facilities provided for conjugal visits, stating that the rooms were too small and too much like prison cells. In spite of these drawbacks, however, the wives felt that the conjugal visits were important for them while their husbands were in prison. They said the visiting program at Parchman was especially helpful in keeping them from worrying so much about their husbands and in allowing them to keep the self-image of being married women. Not a single couple reported an incident in which an inmate or a staff member had acted in a disrespectful manner toward them on visiting day. All would have liked for the visiting hours to have been longer. Half of the wives suggested that the visiting hours should begin at 10 o'clock in the morning instead of 1 o'clock in the afternoon. One suggested that wives be allowed to visit on Saturday and that other visitors have Sunday to themselves.

The sixteen couples discussed above represent the most stable marriages of men in prison; these were marriages that had withstood the prison experience. And some, it seemed, were strengthened by it. Not all wives of men in prison have as much loyalty to their husbands or concern for them as these did. The meaning which conjugal visits have to a wife apparently depends very much upon her general attitude toward her husband. The comment of a wife whose husband was serving his second term in Parchman shows the variation which can occur in the attitude of wives toward conjugal visits. When asked what the conjugal visiting program meant to her, she said that she visited her husband about every two months and added:

I don't really know what it means to me. Well, I guess it does help you remember you are married. It wouldn't really matter to me if they would do away with that [the conjugal visiting privilege]. I would just as soon visit without having it. I just don't believe in B—— so much, and he just really let me down all the way. I just didn't think he would do something like that. I don't know, I just don't think I will ever be able to forget it and what he did to me.

Another wife admitted that she visited her husband only when her mother-in-law came and took her to Parchman. She said that she felt obligated to go since her mother-in-law wanted her to do so. The conjugal visits meant nothing to her, she said, because she no longer cared for her husband. She related that her husband had been "running around" before his commitment, and that she had little hope for a good married life after his release. She added, however, that she thought the conjugal visits should be more private and that the facilities should be cleaner and more modern. Her attitude toward the conjugal visiting program was one of apathy.

A wife who had visited her husband only one time in two years said about the penitentiary in general, "There's nothing I like about it. I guess it's good to have a place like that because you just can't let people run free. I think it's run about as good as it could be considering the kind of people they have up there. The only reason I went to Parchman was just to see the place, to see what the place looked like." She responded to a question about the conjugal visit by saying that her husband had asked her about it on the one occasion she was at Parchman. She said she refused and that he accepted her refusal without any further comment.

Can one conclude that the conjugal visiting program at Parchman is a success? The best evidence is the word of the people involved in it. The officials who administer the program and the inmates and wives who participate in it believe that it has been successful. One long-term staff member had little doubt about the success of the program when he said: "I know one thing for sure, I wouldn't want to be around this place if the conjugal visit was taken away. It would be the greatest blow to the morale of the inmates I can imagine."

Chapter V

Conjugal Visiting and Prisonization

In addition to knowing how staff members and inmates evaluate the conjugal visiting program at Parchman, it is important to consider how the program influences the general prison experience of inmates. Ultimately, any prison program must be assessed in terms of the impact it has on the man himself—on his attitudes toward the law and on his willingness to accept societal authority.

In his study of prisons in England and Wales almost two hundred years ago, John Howard came to know penal institutions as places that functioned virtually as schools in criminality. He realized the unhappy fact that instead of curing the criminal and preventing others from becoming criminals, prisons often rendered the individuals who passed through them more hostile, more bitter, and more deeply entrenched in crime than they were before. Commenting on this Howard said: "In a prison the check of the public eye is removed; and the power of the law is spent. There are few fears, there are few blushes. The lewd inflame the more modest; the audacious harden the timid. Every one fortifies himself as best he can against his own remaining sensibility; endeavoring to practice on others the arts that are practiced on himself; and to gain the applause of his worst associates by imitating their manners." [1]

[1] John Howard, *State of the Prisons in England and Wales* (Warrington, England, 1784), 12.

Although Howard's description of the prisons of his day now seems quaint, the problem he was concerned with still exists in varying degrees in the penal institutions of the present era. Specialists in corrections have become convinced that the experiences which inmates have with one another in the informal social life of prison turn out to be more important than many of the formal programs for rehabilitation set up by prison authorities.

It seems clear that any prison program must be evaluated in the light of how it relates to the informal inmate social system. If a program is to have a positive influence on prisoners, it must have an impact on the relationships they have with each other and with the prison staff members. In studying Parchman, therefore, an attempt was made to compare inmates receiving conjugal visits with those not receiving such visits in terms of their attitudes toward each other and toward the pententiary staff. The theoretical concept used in developing the hypotheses tested in comparing inmates was that developed by Donald Clemmer. Clemmer used the term "prisonization" to indicate the process by which a prisoner adjusts to—and indeed adopts —the folkways, mores, customs, and general culture of a prison. Although the extent to which individuals undergo the process varies; every person sentenced to prison undergoes prisonization to some degree. As Clemmer explained:

> Whether or not complete prisonization takes place depends first on the man himself, that is, his susceptibility to a culture which depends . . . primarily on the type of relationships he had before imprisonment, i.e., his personality. A second determinant effecting complete prisonization refers

to the kind and extent of relationships which an inmate has with persons outside the walls. A third determinant refers to whether or not a man becomes affiliated in primary or semi-primary groups and this is related to the two points already mentioned. Yet a fourth determinant depends simply on chance, a chance placement in work gangs, cellhouse, and with cellmate. A fifth determinant pertains to whether or not a man accepts the dogmas or codes of the prison culture. Other determinants depend on age, criminality, nationality, race, regional conditioning, and every determinant is more or less interrelated with every other one.[2]

The prison itself is a factor in prisonization, but the process goes on in all types of penal institutions. It is, of course, greater in institutions where many men are confined behind walls and bars under constant guard than in minimum security institutions such as Parchman which allow much freedom. Nevertheless, prisonization is not primarily dependent upon the particular structure of a prison but rather upon the relationships between the prisoners and those who control them. The process occurs in chain gangs where prisoners are worked under the gun. Even though they may never be confined in a prison with walls around it, chain gang prisoners still come to hate those who guard them. It is the captive-captor relationship which promotes prisonization, not the shape, size, or organization of a prison.

Prisonization operates even in a plantation penitentiary. A new prisoner at Parchman becomes at once a member of a subordinate group, and he is given a number which re-

[2] Clemmer, *The Prison Community,* 300-301.

places his name. Even though it is now blue denim rather than the traditional stripes, he still must wear the uniform of the group. He is questioned and admonished, and soon learns that the superintendent is all-powerful in his control over the prisoners. The inmate quickly learns the ranks, titles, and authority of the sergeants and other staff members. Whether he uses the Parchman slang and argot or not, he comes to know its meanings as he communicates with other prisoners.

At Parchman, as at any other prison, the inmate is subject to influences which may be called the universal factors or aspects of prisonization. The acceptance of an inferior role; the accumulation of facts concerning the organization of the penitentiary; the development of new habits of eating, sleeping, dressing, and working; the eventual desire for a good job within the institution—all these are aspects of prisonization which he acquires.

However, these are not the only characteristics of the process. The most significant phases of prisonization are the experiences and associations the prisoners have with each other. It is these experiences which breed or deepen criminality and make an individual accept the negativistic ideology found in prison. While all inmates feel the influences of the universal factors, not every inmate comes to completely identify with his fellow convicts and accept society's designation of himself as a criminal. Some prisoners cooperate with the staff members and try to improve their status within the inmate classification system.

The lowest grade inmate at Parchman is known as a "gunman." Gunmen are prisoners who must be guarded

at all times. They wear blue denim trousers with a white
stripe running the full length of each leg. The next highest
grade is half-trusty. Half-trusties are usually called "legs."
They are not guarded during the day but are locked up
with the gunmen at night. "Legs" wear blue denim trousers with a white stripe running halfway down each leg.
The highest grade an inmate may have is the position of
trusty. Trusties wear solid white trousers. There are also a
small number of men known as "riskies." A risky is a man
who has committed an unusually heinous crime which
makes him ineligible to become a trusty. If such a man
becomes a well-behaved prisoner, he is made a risky with
privileges similar to the half-trusty. He wears the clothes
of a gunman, however, and is simply known by the staff
members as a prisoner who is in the risky category.

An important indication that a Parchman inmate has
acquired the deleterious aspects of prisonization is his
acceptance of the role and values of the hard-core gunmen.
When he accepts the value system of the worst gunmen—
or, as inmates at Parchman say, when he becomes a "hog"
and begins to "think" like a gunman—he is well along in
the prisonization process. This means that he has stopped
thinking of himself as an individual and that he has accepted the self-image of a man who is dangerous enough
to require constant guard. He accepts his status as a hog
and draws a sharp distinction between the free world people and the prisoners. Not only does a prisonized inmate
make a distinction between himself and the free people,
he comes to hate the free society and especially the ser-

geants and drivers who represent the authority of that society.

The value system of prisonized inmates takes the form of an explicit code which guides the behavior of a hog in his relationships with his fellow inmates and his custodians.. The chief tenets of the inmate code are: [3]

(1) *Don't interfere with inmate interests.* The most inflexible directive in this regard is concerned with the betrayal of a fellow prisoner to the penitentiary officials. Prisoners, this part of the code contends, must present a unified front against the institutional staff no matter how much this may cost in terms of personal sacrifice. Cooperation with the free world people is not tolerated by a hog. He has, rather, only contempt and hostility toward prisoners with a cooperative attitude toward the penitentiary staff.

(2) *Don't lose your head.* A man who is prisonized has control of his emotions. He "plays it cool" and "rolls with the punches." He does not expect a good break and can withstand such things as being turned down for a parole without losing his head. He ignores the irritants of prison life and "does his own time."

(3) *Don't weaken.* This directive places emphasis upon the ability to withstand frustration or threatening situations without complaints or resorting to subservience. A hog is able to "take it" and to maintain a stoic integrity in

---

[3] For further discussion of the inmate code, see Gresham Sykes and Sheldon L. Messinger, "The Inmate Social Code and Its Functions," in Norman Johnson and others (eds.), *The Sociology of Punishment and Correction* (New York, 1963), 92–98.

the face of privation. If a man is thoroughly prisonized his attitude is: "Whatever those lousy drivers can dish out, I can take." He can even take "Black Annie," the whip, without begging for mercy. He does not fear being sent to Maximum Security, nor does he complain if he is put in the "hole."

(4) *Don't exploit inmates.* This imperative sums up several directives such as "Don't break your word" and "Don't steal from the cons." Positively, it is understood that the inmates should share goods in a balanced reciprocity. Above all, a man following the inmate code would not use another inmate to his own advantage or let a prisoner down who was depending on him. However, the inmate code is followed by "right guys" and not by all prisoners. "Right guys" are the inmates who stick together, and a man has to earn his way into the fold. Thus, right guys may abuse a new inmate or rape a boy unmercifully, and still hold to the notion of "honor" for the other right guys.

(5) *Don't be a sucker.* This maxim forbids the according of prestige or respect to the penitentiary staff members. The sergeants and other personnel are to be treated with suspicion and distrust. In any situation of conflict between officials and prisoners, the officials are automatically to be considered in the wrong. Furthermore, hogs do not become committed to the values of hard work emphasized at Parchman. They do as little as they can get by with, and they do it grudgingly. Under no circumstances does an inmate trust a staff member when he is following the inmate code. He believes that a sergeant, or anyone else in the free

world, who offers to help him has some motive other than sincerity. He looks upon the new vocational programs as "hogwash" and shuns the opportunities for self-improvement.

The thoroughly prisonized inmate, therefore, gives strong verbal support to and possesses attitudes indicative of a system of values that has inmate cohesion or solidarity as its basic theme. He sees prisoners as firmly united in their opposition to the enemy out-group, the staff members. He uses, in all situations, the inmate code as a guide in his relationships with staff members and prisoners.

Does the conjugal visiting program have any effect on a prisoner's acceptance of the inmate code? This question formed a significant reason for undertaking the present study of Parchman's unique program. For if conjugal visits have a positive influence on a prisoner, he should be less bound by the code. Therefore, inmates who received the visits were compared with those who did not as to whether they accepted the code's major tenets. To obtain such findings, the following hypotheses were tested:

(1) Inmates who receive conjugal visits will agree less often on loyalty among prisoners than inmates who do not engage in conjugal visits.

(2) Inmates who receive conjugal visits will be more favorable to working hard at their prison jobs than will inmates who do not engage in conjugal visits.

(3) Inmates who receive conjugal visits will be more favorable to cooperating with the staff of the penitentiary than prisoners who do not engage in conjugal visits.

(4) Inmates who receive conjugal visits will be more

willing to trust the staff of the penitentiary than prisoners who do not engage in conjugal visits.

(5) Inmates who receive conjugal visits will trust other prisoners less than those who do not receive conjugal visits.

(6) Inmates who receive conjugal visits will view the staff of the penitentiary as being fairer in dealings with prisoners than will those who do not receive conjugal visits.

(7) Inmates who receive conjugal visits will have fewer close friends among prisoners than will those who do not receive conjugal visits.

(8) Among inmates who receive conjugal visits, the differences hypothesized above will vary directly with the frequency of their conjugal visits.

To obtain data for testing the hypotheses, the prisoners were asked to fill out a questionnaire in which they could agree or disagree with statements based upon the tenets of the inmate code. The chief aim in choosing inmates for study was to collect questionnaires from as nearly all of the prisoners as possible in order to assure a satisfactory sampling of those who did and those who did not receive conjugal visits.

In October, 1963, there were 2,223 inmates on record at the penitentiary. From that total, it was necessary to make deletions in order to compare prisoners under equal conditions receiving and not receiving conjugal visits. First, those in camps not having conjugal visiting privileges had to be eliminated. Thus female inmates did not fill out questionnaires. Also, the small number of prisoners in the Maximum Security unit were not contacted, nor were those in the hospital at Parchman, nor in the state mental hospital at Whitfield. In addition, 10 inmates on duty in the Governor's Mansion at Jackson were left out of the study. Altogether, those in camps not having conjugal visiting privileges numbered 170, leaving a total of 2,053 men confined in camps which did allow the privilege. From this number, 1,765 questionnaires were collected, leaving a total of 288 prisoners missed. Of those missed, most were on duty as trusty guards or on work assignment. A few were asbsent on emergency leaves; others, although not seriously ill, complained of headaches or some such trouble and requested to be allowed to remain in the sleeping quarters while the questionnaire was administered. A total of 164 questionnaires were not complete enough to be usable and were also eliminated. The final group comprised 77.9 percent of the prison population confined in camps which allowed conjugal visits. In the group studied, there were 465 men receiving conjugal visits and 1,136 men who were not receiving the visits. (See Table 4.)

To facilitate the administration of the questionnaire, inmates were asked to go to the dining hall and be seated at the table as at meal time. Before the questionnaires were handed out, a statement was made by the researcher. The prisoners were told that the study was being made for purely scientific purposes in order to learn more about the experience of going to prison and what it means to the individual inmate. They were told not to put their names or prison numbers on the questionnaires, and they were assured that the information they gave would remain anonymous and would in no way either help them or hurt them. In order to help the inmates understand the process

Table 4

STATISTICAL BREAKDOWN OF MEN
WHO ANSWERED QUESTIONNAIRES

Category	Number
White married men receiving conjugal visits	124
White married men not receiving visits	95
Negro married men receiving conjugal visits	341
Negro married men not receiving visits	215
White single men	148
Negro single men	384
White divorced men	111
Negro divorced men	105
White widowers	18
Negro widowers	60
Total white men	496
Total Negro men	1,105
Grand total of men answering questionnaires	1,601

involved, each question with its possible answers was read to them. This procedure was also employed to keep down the number of unusable questionnaires.

In constructing the questionnaires, the basic concern was to develop questions which would allow a comparison of those who responded relative to their participation in and reliance upon the inmate social system. And since the essential concern of the concept of prisonization is the attitude of the inmate, rather than his behavior, it seemed most profitable to make the majority of the questions relate to attitudes rather than to reports of actual behavior. While behavior is the thing of immediate prominence in the in-

mate's interaction in the penitentiary, the emotional acceptance of the norms themselves as principles is the
enduring component of the prison experience. An inmate
may physically conform to staff expectations without open
conflict and yet will still come out of the institution highly
prisonized. Thus, most of the questions did not call for a
delineation of the individual's participation, but rather for
his acceptance or rejection of the norms of the social system
as expressed in the inmate code. In order to cause the
prisoners as little trouble as possible in deciding on their
answers, the norms, or tenets of the code, were stated briefly
and generally and the inmates were asked only to agree or
disagree with them as statements of principles. Agreement to a statement like "Staff members should never be
trusted" was believed to reflect more truly the inmate's
lasting experiences than whether or not he would trust any
individual staff member to help him with a specific problem or in a specific hypothetical instance.

Five hypotheses were tested, therefore, by comparing the
agreement of the inmates to a normative statement associated with each hypothesis. Another hypothesis was tested
by comparing the rating of fairness of the staff members.
An additional hypothesis was tested by comparing the
number of close friends the inmates reported. A final
hypothesis was tested by comparing the number of close
friends within the group of inmates who received conjugal
visits with the frequency of the visits held constant. These
hypotheses were all tested by the chi square test of significance, a simple contingency measure designed to determine whether the difference between the expected and the

observed frequencies are greater than chance variation.

Inmate loyalty. The most inflexible tenet of the inmate code is that of loyalty. It demands that prisoners present a unified front against the penitentiary staff members. The first hypothesis tested, therefore, concerned the dogma of loyalty. Prisoners were asked whether they agreed with the following statement: "Above all, inmates should stick together and be loyal to each other."

The difference in agreement of men receiving conjugal visits and those not receiving conjugal visits was less than 1 percent and not statistically significant. Approximately 73 percent of both groups agreed with the statement.[4] Those receiving conjugal visits were, in fact, a little more in agreement to the maxim of loyalty than most other groups when compared by marital status. Only single prisoners had a higher percentage (79.3) of agreement. Divorced and widowed men agreed least, with 68.5 percent and 65.4 percent, respectively.

Since single prisoners are on the average younger than other inmates, it is possible that the age of inmates makes a difference in their agreement to loyalty. The men were therefore grouped into those twenty-five years old or less, twenty-six to forty, and forty-one and over. While younger men were more likely to agree with the statement of inmate loyalty, there were no statistically significant differences between inmates receiving conjugal visits and other inmates in the three age groups compared.

Since the type of work a prisoner may do within the

---

[4] The exact figures were 72.9 percent of inmates receiving conjugal visits and 73.8 percent of those not receiving such visits.

penitentiary varies basically in only two respects—field work and other work such as maintenance, clerical, and mechanical—the prisoners were grouped into those working as field hands and those working at other jobs. Although field hands agreed more than other prisoners, those receiving conjugal visits did not differ significantly from other prisoners in either group. When race was held constant, the differences between inmates receiving conjugal visits and other inmates still were not significant. Race was a factor, however, in agreement to inmate loyalty. The overall agreement of Negroes was 14.8 percent higher than that of the white prisoners.

Although the prisoners were compared with prior commitments, time served, and education held constant, no significant variation occurred. Most of the analysis showed, rather, a remarkable similarity between men receiving conjugal visits and the rest of the prisoners.

Inmate work. If a prisoner does more than he is forced to do on his job in the penitentiary, he is a sucker in the eyes of those who follow the inmate code. Rather than working hard at his job, the hog strives to be "sharp," to get a "connection." The prominence of work in the prisoner's life at Parchman places this aspect of the code in a position of importance. One of the surest signs that an individual is departing from the inmate code is for him to have a positive attitude toward working hard at his job. As another indication of their allegiance to the inmate code, therefore, prisoners at Parchman were asked to agree or disagree with the following statement: "An inmate should work as hard as he can at his job in the penitentiary."

Table 5

AGREEMENT TO WORKING HARD:
Inmates Receiving Conjugal Visits Compared to Inmates
Not Receiving Conjugal Visits by Marital Status

Agreement to Working Hard	Inmates Receiving Conjugal Visits		Married Inmates Not Receiving Conjugal Visits		Single	
	No.	%	No.	%	No.	%
Agree	386	83.0	222	71.4	347	65.3
Disagree	79	17.0	89	28.6	184	34.7
Total	465	100.0	311	100.0	531*	100.0

Agreement to Working Hard	Divorced		Widowed		Total
	No.	%	No.	%	
Agree	141	65.3	62	80.5	1158
Disagree	75	34.7	15	19.5	442
Total	216	100.0	77	100.0	1600*

X^2 (4 df) 47.5707 P
* One inmate did not answer this question. Therefore, totals differ from other tables.

Those receiving conjugal visits had a significantly higher percentage of agreement. Eighty-three percent of the men receiving conjugal visits agreed to the statement as compared to 68 percent of the other prisoners. When inmates receiving conjugal visits were compared to each marital status category, as shown in Table 5, the differences were statistically significant for all comparisons except with widowed prisoners.

With jobs held constant, the difference between men receiving and not receiving conjugal visits remained significant, although it was apparent that men working as field hands were less likely to agree to working hard. Among field hands, there was a 16.8 percent difference between those receiving conjugal visits and other inmates. Among the men working at other jobs, the difference was only 9.5 percent.

When Negro and white inmates were compared separately, the differences remained significant, although the difference between white inmates was greater than the difference between the Negro prisoners. With race and job factors both held constant, three of the four subgroups retained significant differences. Among Negro men working at jobs other than field work, however, those receiving conjugal visits did not agree more than the others. It appears, therefore, that the type of job the inmate had in the penitentiary was related as strongly to agreement to working hard by Negro men as was conjugal visiting. Among white men, however, conjugal visiting was more related to agreement to working hard than the type of work the inmate did.

When age was considered, the differences between inmates receiving conjugal visits and other inmates were still significant. While there was a tendency for older men to agree more to working hard, the youngest group of prisoners receiving conjugal visits agreed more than the oldest group not receiving conjugal visits. The differences between inmates receiving conjugal visits and other inmates were significant in all four educational levels examined.[5] Even though those who received conjugal visits were compared to other prisoners under varied subgroup

[5] The levels of schooling were: Four years or less; five to seven years; eight to eleven; and twelve years or more.

analysis, they continued to be higher in agreement to working hard than were the other prisoners.

Cooperation with the staff. The thoroughly prisonized inmate should be able to "take it." He should not compromise his defiance to the penitentiary staff members. Whatever he does at the direction of the staff should be done in a manner which leaves no doubt of his lack of commitment to the act. Thus the prisoners at Parchman were asked if they agreed with the following statement: "An inmate should cooperate with the staff of the penitentiary." Those who received conjugal visits had 13.6 percent higher agreement than did the other prisoners, a difference which is statistically significant. Of those receiving conjugal visits, 82.9 percent agreed to the statement as compared to 69.2 percent of the other prisoners. When compared to all other men by marital status, those receiving conjugal visits had a higher percentage of agreement than any other group.

When race was held constant, as shown in Table 6, the differences remained significant, but it was evident that more Negroes than whites agreed with the statement. Overall, Negroes had a 23.3 percent higher agreement. The relationship between conjugal visiting and agreement to cooperation also appeared to be different among white and Negro inmates when the job factor was held constant. The highest percentage of agreement (90.1) occurred among Negro men receiving conjugal visits and working at jobs other than field work; the lowest agreement (55.4 percent) was among white men not receiving conjugal visits and working as field hands.

The older inmates were more favorable to cooperating with staff members than were younger prisoners. The length of time served was also found to be related to attitudes toward cooperation. No significant differences were found among those having served less than one year whether or not they received conjugal visits. Of those

Table 6
AGREEMENT TO COOPERATING WITH THE STAFF: Inmates Receiving Conjugal Visits Compared to Inmates Not Receiving Conjugal Visits with Race Held Constant

Agreement to Cooperating With Staff	Inmates Receiving Conjugal Visits		Inmates Not Receiving Conjugal Visits		Total
		White[a]			
	No.	%	No.	%	
Agree	83	66.9	195	52.4	278
Disagree	41	33.1	177	47.6	218
Total	124	100.0	372	100.0	496

X^2 (1 df) 7.9551 P < .01[a]

		Negro[b]			
Agree	302	88.5	590	77.3	892
Disagree	39	11.5	173	22.7	212
Total	341	100.0	763*	100.0	1104*

X^2 (1 df) 19.1789 P < .001[b]
*One inmate not answering question.

who had served more than one year, however, those not having conjugal visits were less likely to feel that they should cooperate with the staff. The difference was especially great for those who had served more than two years.

Trust in staff. To the prisonized, guards and other staff members are to be treated with constant suspicion and distrust. Among the "prison-wise," the easiest way to make a fool of oneself is to trust a staff member. As a test of the fourth hypothesis, prisoners at Parchman had to agree or disagree with the following statement: "Prison staff members should never be trusted."

As may be seen in Table 7, the prisoners who received conjugal visits disagreed more frequently, and the hypothesis was supported. When compared to all others by marital status, those receiving conjugal visits disagreed to a greater extent. Race did not appear to be an important factor. Although men working as field hands agreed 11.6 percent more than prisoners in other jobs, the difference between inmates receiving conjugal visits and others remained. There was also a tendency for inmates with more education to disagree more.

Table 7

AGREEMENT TO DISTRUSTING STAFF MEMBERS: Inmates Receiving Conjugal Visits Compared to Inmates Not Receiving Conjugal Visits

Agreement to Distrusting Staff Members	Inmates Receiving Conjugal Visits		Inmates Not Receiving Conjugal Visits		Total
	No.	%	No.	%	
Agree	165	35.5	535	47.1	700
Disagree	300	64.5	601	52.9	901
Total	465	100.0	1136	100.0	1601

X^2 (1 df) 18.0781 P < .001

Statistical significance was retained in each of the three age groups compared. Controlling for prior commitments, however, revealed that no significant difference existed among inmates with two or more prior commitments even though they did receive conjugal visits.

Trust in inmate friends. The inmates were asked how much they trusted their inmate friends. In answering they chose one of five possible answers: (1) "I completely trust them," (2) "I almost completely trust them," (3) "I generally trust them," (4) "I generally do not trust them," (5) "I never trust them." Answers to this question did not vary significantly. As Table 8 shows, the answers of the men receiving conjugal visits were remarkably similar to

Table 8

TRUST IN INMATE FRIENDS: Inmates Receiving Conjugal Visits Compared to Inmates Not Receiving Conjugal Visits

Trust in Inmate Friends	Inmates Receiving Conjugal Visits		Inmates Not Receiving Conjugal Visits		Total
	No.	%	No.	%	
Completely Trust	63	13.5	215	18.9	278
Almost Completely Trust	48	10.3	134	11.8	182
Generally Trust	152	32.7	326	28.7	478
Generally Do Not Trust	78	16.8	170	15.0	248
Never Trust	124	26.7	291	25.6	415
Total	465	100.0	1136	100.0	1601

X^2 (4 df) 8.7261 Not Significant

those of the other prisoners. When white and Negro prisoners were compared separately, the difference between those receiving and not receiving conjugal visits remained insignificant. Negro inmates, however, trusted other Negro inmates more than white prisoners did other white prisoners.

The length of time served did not influence the prisoners' answers. Contrary to expectation, men who were first-termers trusted their friends more than did those who had served time previously. Prisoners above the age of forty trusted their inmate friends more than did the men younger than forty. Another interesting finding was that among prisoners who had twelve years or more education those receiving conjugal visits trusted their inmate friends significantly more than did the men not having such visits.

Rating of fairness of staff. The man exhibiting a high degree of prisonization and loyalty to the inmate code not only distrusts prison staff members, but also believes them to be unfair in their dealings with inmates. Thus the prisoners at Parchman were asked: "How would you rate the staff of this institution in terms of their fairness to inmates?" In answering, the prisoners chose one of the following statements: "They are very fair," "They are generally fair," "They are generally unfair," "They are very unfair."

The expectation was that inmates who received conjugal visits would rate the staff as being fairer than would those not receiving conjugal visits and, as Table 9 shows, the figures bore this out. Those receiving conjugal visits had a higher percentage of fair ratings than did any other group compared by marital status. Race, however, importantly influenced the answers. Conjugal visiting did not make a difference in the answers of the white prisoners, but among Negroes the difference in those receiving conjugal visits and other inmates remained. The overall rating of staff fairness given by Negroes was 13.9 percent higher than the overall rating from whites, in spite of the fact that all of the staff members are white.

Table 9

STAFF FAIRNESS RATING: Inmates Receiving Conjugal Visits Compared to Inmates Not Receiving Conjugal Visits

Staff Fairness Rating	Inmates Receiving Conjugal Visits		Inmates Not Receiving Conjugal Visits		Total
	No.	%	No.	%	
Very Fair	235	50.5	484	42.6	719
Generally Fair	154	33.1	360	31.7	514
Generally Unfair	26	5.6	102	9.0	128
Very Unfair	50	10.8	189	16.7	239
Total	465	100.0	1135*	100.0	1600*

X^2 (3 df) 17.2638 P < .001
*One inmate not answering question.

Nonfield workers rated the staff as being fairer than did field workers. First offenders gave the highest rating of staff fairness among inmates not receiving conjugal visits as well as among those receiving conjugal visits. Generally speaking, the highest ratings of staff fairness came from men with the least education; at all educational levels, however, those receiving conjugal visits saw the staff as being fairer.

Number of inmate friends. Although the number of friends a person has—in or out of prison—is to a large extent a matter of his personality, it was hypothesized that prisoners who received conjugal visits would be less likely to identify with other inmates and would therefore report having fewer friends among prisoners. As a test of this hypothesis, the prisoners were asked how many close friends they had among the inmates at Parchman. In analysis, they were grouped into those having four or less, five to ten, and eleven or more.

As indicated in Table 10, there was a significant difference in the number of close friends reported by the prisoners. The difference, however, was not in the expected direction. Inmates receiving conjugal visits had not less but more friends than other prisoners. For both groups of prisoners, the largest percentage was in the group having four or less friends. The second largest percentage for both groups was in the group having eleven or more close friends, reflecting a tendency to have either a few friends or many friends.

Race influenced friendship patterns. There was no difference in white prisoners who received conjugal visits and white men who did not. Among Negro men, however, those who received conjugal visits had significantly more close friends. Negroes had more close friends in general than did whites. The men with the fewest friends were white field workers; of these, 74.1 percent had fewer than five close friends. The men with the most friends were Negro prisoners who worked as nonfield hands; of these, only 44.3 percent had fewer than five close friends.

Table 10

NUMBER OF INMATE FRIENDS: Inmates Receiving Conjugal
Visits Compared to Inmates Not Receiving Conjugal Visits

Number of Inmate Friends	Inmates Receiving Conjugal Visits		Inmates Not Receiving Conjugal Visits		Total
	No.	%	No.	%	
Four or Less	251	53.9	700	61.6	251
Five to Ten	76	16.3	163	14.3	239
Eleven or More	138	29.7	273	24.0	411
Total	465	100.0	1136	100.0	1601

X^2 (2 df) 8.2199 P $<$ .02

In overall comparison, those over forty years of age had most friends. Among prisoners having served less than one year, the friendship patterns were very similar whether or not they received conjugal visits. All prisoners had more close friends if they had served more than one year; among those receiving conjugal visits, however, the difference was more pronounced.

Only research designed specifically around friendship patterns of prisoners at Parchman can determine whether or not the inmates receiving conjugal visits have their friends among other inmates who also receive conjugal visits. If this pattern exists, however, it is probably true only among Negroes, since white prisoners who receive conjugal visits did not have more friends than other white prisoners.

The fact that inmates receiving conjugal visits had more friends than other prisoners should not necessarily be interpreted in an unfavorable manner. Although one line of reasoning leads one to believe that inmates with strong positive relations with family members in the free community will develop fewer friends in prison, the friendship patterns in a prison community, like any other community, are very complicated The greater number of friends among those receiving conjugal visits can just as easily be viewed as an indication of their better social adjustment and their ability to develop stable and satisfying social relationships generally.

Frequency of conjugal visits. If conjugal visits are a factor in the inmates' relationships within the penitentiary, a reasonable expectation is that the men who receive the most frequent visits will give more indication of the influence than inmates who receive the visits less often. The foregoing hypotheses, therefore, were examined with the frequency of the visit utilized as a control within the group of prisoners who received conjugal visits. In only two of the seven hypotheses did the frequency of the visit have an influence. The two that were influenced, however, were two that had previously been unsupported. Table 11 shows that of those receiving conjugal visits once a month or oftener, 50.9 percent trusted their inmate friends as compared to 65.6 percent of those receiving conjugal visits less than once a month. The number of close friends was also related to the frequency of conjugal visits. Of those receiving conjugal visits once a month or more often, 60 percent had four or less close friends; of those receiving the visits less than once a month, only 44.4 percent had four or less friends.

Table 11

TRUST IN INMATE FRIENDS: Inmates Receiving Conjugal Visits Grouped Into Those Receiving Visits Once a Month or More and Less Than Once a Month

Trust in Inmate Friends	Inmates Receiving Conjugal Visits Once a Month or More		Inmates Receiving Conjugal Visits Less Than Once a Month		Total
	No.	%	No.	%	
Trust	145	50.9	118	65.6	263
Do Not Trust	140	49.1	62	34.4	202
Total	285	100.0	180	100.0	465

X^2 (1 df) 9.6742 P < .01

Of the seven hypotheses relating to the effect conjugal visits had on prisonization in the penitentiary, four were supported and three were not supported. Those supported had to do with: agreement to working hard; cooperating with the staff; trust in staff members; and ratings of the fairness of staff members. Those not supported had to do with: loyalty among inmates; trust in inmate friends; and the number of inmate friends. Generally speaking, the hypotheses break down into a rather clear pattern of those supported and not supported. Those relating to the inmate's interaction with other inmates were not supported; those relating to the inmate's interaction with the staff members were. Inmates who received conjugal visits, thus, did give indication that they had more positive relationships with the staff of the institution. They did not give indication, however, of having less positive relationships with other inmates.

It is interesting to note that the frequency of the conjugal visits made a difference only among those hypotheses relating to the inmate's relationships to other inmates. Such an outcome, however, seems logical. By the granting of the privilege, the staff has done as much as it can. The frequency of the visit is not dependent upon the staff members, and the prisoners recognize this. Consequently, a prisoner who receives a conjugal visit only once every two months may still be as favorable to the staff as those receiving visits more often; he has the knowledge that the staff members would allow the privilege on every visiting day if the inmate and his wife could manage it.

The only hypothesis which did not seem influenced in some way by the practice of conjugal visiting concerned loyalty among inmates. Apparently, this dogma of the inmate code is the strongest of all and the most severely sanctioned. Inmates who receive conjugal visits still have to live among inmates. The person who betrays group trust or loyalty is not a popular individual even on the outside of prison. In the prison community, an individual who does not respect the maxim of loyalty places his life in real danger. Inmates who receive conjugal visits, as all inmates, must be loyal if they are to survive.

Chapter VI

A Look to the Future

What lessons may be drawn, then, from the Mississippi State Penitentiary's experiment with conjugal visiting? And what of future developments in conjugal visiting programs, at Parchman and elsewhere in the United States? What have the findings of the survey and interviews of 1963 shown? What has this study as a whole accomplished? Perhaps it will be best to examine the answers to the above questions in reverse order so that the reader may go from facts to conjecturings on the future possibilities and may thus draw his own conclusions.

This study has had three major purposes: first, to present a true picture of the Mississippi State Penitentiary and the program of conjugal visiting as it has developed through the years and as it now exists; second, to relate conjugal visiting to the social organization of the prison; and finally, to examine how conjugal visiting relates to the acquisition of the dominant norms, or tenets, of the inmate code. As has been pointed out, Parchman's five unique organizational features with the important factors in the evolution of conjugal visiting. These five were: the rural environment of the penitentiary; the plantation system it is based upon; the economic motives of the institution; the small-camp arrangement in housing inmates; and the segregation of the races within the penitentiary.

Probably the most important conclusion to be drawn

137

from the findings of the questionnaires and the inmates answers is the necessity for future research projects which would embody aspects of a more experimental design. Although the findings reported here indicated that prisoners who received conjugal visits differed significantly from other inmates in several aspects of their relationships to the staff members at Parchman, it may not now be concluded that these differences were due entirely to the practice of conjugal visiting. It may instead be argued, for example, that the differences found are merely reflections of the more stable personalities of men whose marriages have remained intact, and that their responses would have been the same even if they had not received conjugal visits. Consequently, a more meaningful study to ascertain the actual influence of the visits might employ a "before and after" technique. Studies should be made of the prisoners when they first arrive at the penitentiary in order to get a better indication of the differences between the inmates before exposure to either actual incarceration or to conjugal visits. Additional studies at intervals throughout a man's entire confinement would more satisfactorily compare those who receive and those who do not receive the visits.

In spite of the limitations of the data reported, the differences found between the men receiving conjugal visits and other prisoners in the Mississippi State Penitentiary actually seem rather remarkable in view of the conditions under which the program has been operating. Prisoners who receive conjugal visits have not received any special consideration from the penitentiary officials. No systematic counseling has been given, nor has any selection of prisoners who receive visits been made other than the criterion of marriage. Obviously, therefore, the practice of conjugal visiting would seem to have at least some positive potential in other prisons with structural and organizational practices conducive to the program.

It should be emphasized, however, that one may not safely generalize from the Mississippi experience in regard to other prisons across the country. As the research has indicated, the success of conjugal visiting at Parchman may be dependent upon general and specific features of the penitentiary itself. These features are not to be found in the great majority of penal institutions in the United States. While the Mississippi penitentiary is located in a rural state and serves a rural population, most of the other prisons in this country are not rural in either sense. The plantation system is also a system more associated with the past than with the future in the United States. Modern correctional authorities do not view a prison as an economic institution. Nor are correctional personnel apt to endorse a pattern of segregating racial or ethnic groups to circumvent whatever taboos might exist in regard to their interaction. Most of the organizational factors believed to be importantly associated with conjugal visiting in Mississippi, therefore, are factors which may have little relevance to other penal institutions in this country.

On the other hand, it should not be concluded that conjugal visiting should be ruled out for other American penitentiaries simply because they do not possess the same organizational characteristics as Parchman does. It is possible that a program of conjugal visitation could operate even more successfully in another prison of a different type. The organizational features cited above are those which were most important in allowing the development of conjugal visiting in Mississippi, but its successful operation is more dependent upon the small-camp structure used in housing prisoners. It is likely that small camps or units would remain fundamental to a program of conjugal visiting regardless of the cultural area in which the prison operated.

The small-unit arrangement of housing inmates offers much opportunity for experimentation in all forms of visitation as well as conjugal visiting. Most importantly, the small camps allow staff members to become personally acquainted with the prisoners and to develop close relationships with them. One of the most significant aspects of the data presented was that the majority of all inmates in the Mississippi State Penitentiary, whether or not they received conjugal visits, were favorable to the staff of the penitentiary. It is likely that the overall favorable evaluation by the inmates is a result of the close relationships that the size of the camps allow.

The staff members and the inmates at Parchman come to know each other well because the numbers are small and they are able to operate on the basis of primary relationships. The small-camp arrangement, therefore, has great potential for the whole process of rehabilitation. If rehabilitation comes to prisoners, it is basically through the relationships they have with staff members. The structure of a penal institution, consequently, is of fundamental importance. A prison structure which does not allow the staff and inmates close interaction is not likely to develop a meaningful program of rehabilitation. Although rehabilitative programs have been emphasized but a short time in Mississippi, the relationships which have been developed in the penitentiary hold much potential in this regard. A penal institution in which the majority of inmates believe the staff members are fair and are willing to trust them and to cooperate with them is one which has made the most difficult breakthrough in the rehabilitative process—the attainment of a positive relationship between inmates and staff members.

Facilities for the conjugal visits remain a big problem at Parchman. Staff members, inmates, and wives of inmates all rated the red houses currently being used as very unsatisfactory. Certainly a program such as Parchman's which shows so much positive potential with neglected facilities should be give more financial and institutional support. With better facilities, careful selection of inmates who may participate, and appropriate counseling, it is possible that the conjugal visiting program in Mississippi could be developed into one of the most enlightened programs in modern correctional institutions.

The experience in Mississippi calls for serious consideration and evaluation—particularly since Parchman, the only institution in the United States in which conjugal visiting is fully operative, considers the program important and successful enough to include visiting facilities in future building and construction plans. This fact may well indicate that conjugal visiting, at least in certain types of institutions, can be developed into not only an acceptable practice but one which has positive merit as well. In spite of whatever progress is made in allowing inmates to take furloughs from the prison, most penologists are not optimistic in believing that the day will soon come when a significant proportion of prisoners will be able to enjoy this privilege. For most inmates, prisons will remain "total" institutions which confine them twenty-four hours a day.

It is altogether feasible that what is unrealistic in one prison system might be a satisfactory arrangement in another system differently constructed and differently operated. In any event, the point to be considered here is that the conjugal visit appears to have become an important and respected part of the system in the Mississippi State Penitentiary. This fact alone seems to warrant the conclusion that conjugal visiting should be studied not only in comparison with but also in conjunction with other types of visiting programs in a variety of institutions. Parchman's experience does not prove that the objections to conjugal visiting are invalid; it suggests, however, that conjugal visiting, at least in some penal situations, cannot be ruled out as a possible adaptation in American penology.

Mississippi's experiment with conjugal visiting also implies that the practice should not continue to be disfavored in American prisons chiefly on moral grounds. Although conjugal visits may have been unrealistic in the United States in an earlier Puritan era, it is equally unrealistic to reject the practice as being against current mores in America. The penal administrators who object to the sexual emphasis in conjugal visits probably represent the most conservative elements of the American public. Many, perhaps even the majority of Americans, now accept sex as a natural part of human existence. There is now an emphasis on sexual campatibility within marriage. The sexual theme in American marriage may be developing to the point that it will soon be considered improper to deny both husband and wife the "rights of marriage" when the husband is in prison.

It should again be emphasized here that the small unit system utilized in Mississippi is the most important aspect of the institution in relation to the apparent success in the controversial conjugal visiting program. The objections to the practice expressed by most penologists are very real and formidable for the typical state prison in this country. And there are also formidable objections, and even less likelihood of conjugal visiting ever becoming part of the rehabilitation programs, in federal prisons. One factor here would be the distance most of the inmates' wives would have to travel in order to visit their husbands serving sentences in a federal prison. As stated before, where the wives live plays an important role in the success of the program at Parchman. One wife interviewed said that a distance of two hundred miles made it very difficult for her to visit her husband and that their children had not been able to do so at all. But even more important is the fact that most prisons are so large and house so many inmates in one central building that security precautions must always be paramount in their operation. Undoubtedly conjugal visiting could prove quite embarrassing in a prison where many inmates would wish to use the facilities at one time. A large prison would not allow the informal, relaxed security precautions extant in Parchman.

The greatest lesson to be learned from Mississippi's experience in conjugal visiting, therefore, is not that the objections to the practice are spurious but that prisons in the United States confine too many inmates in mass cell blocks. Mass cell block systems will always have most emphasis on security and will remain unwieldly and resistant to change—particularly change which depends for its success on cooperation and trust between inmates and staff.

The outlook for conjugal visiting at Parchman seems brighter now than it ever has. Along with his plans to improve other aspects of the program, Superintendent Cook hopes to improve the buildings used for conjugal visits. "If we are going to have conjugal visiting," he told the author in January of 1969, "we need to do something about the old buildings. Some of them are really in bad shape. I want all of the buildings at the penitentiary to look good, to be something we can be proud of." Cook wants Parchman to become a model penal institution in conjugal visiting as well as in vocational training. He believes that improved facilities will give the program a much better image and make other penologists more willing to develop similar practices.

Before conjugal visits can be accepted on a wide scale in other American penal institutions, however, a basic change must be made in penal philosophy. Although carefully disguised, the objections of most prison administrators to conjugal visiting seem, in large part, restatements of the old philosophy that criminals are sentenced to prison for punishment, not for treatment. For example, most penologists want to develop a furlough system rather than conjugal visiting. Although they realize that something needs to be done about sexual problems in prison, their emphasis upon leaves rather than conjugal visits indicates that they do not want much change within the institutions themselves. They are willing to allow selected inmates the privilege of leaving the institutions for brief periods, but are unwilling to do away with the sexually deprived conditions of inmates within the walls.

The argument that conjugal visits do not meet the needs of all prisoners is unsound and reflects the same bias. One might argue against a furlough system or any other practice on the same grounds. No one has proposed a furlough system which applies to all inmates categorically. Penal administrators must likewise stop rejecting conjugal visits because they are not a complete answer to sex problems in prison. It must be realized that the problem is going to continue to exist in some degree as long as there are prisons. We cannot, however, afford to reject something which helps the problem even a little. It is unwise to deny a minority of prisoners conjugal visits because all cannot have them. It is as foolish to reject conjugal visits on this basis as it would be to reject a vocational training program because not all inmates wanted to take advantage of it or could not qualify for it. What is needed, of course, is not leaves instead of conjugal visits, but *both leaves and conjugal visits.* Many new developments are needed, not just one. Conjugal visiting has a place in a prison along with leaves, counseling, and educational and vocational training.

As its critics argue, conjugal visiting may have relatively little effect on the biological needs of prisoners. Under current visiting regulations in most prisons, the conjugal visit could not occur often enough to significantly reduce the sexual needs of those participating in such a program. *What it would influence, however, is the image of a man.* It would allow a man to keep his masculine image and reduce the need to establish it through homosexual conquests.

Unfortunately, most prison administrators still see homosexuality in prison as a biological problem rather than as a social or psychological problem. Most of them view homosexuality in prison as a direct result of the deprivation of sexual (heterosexual) intercourse itself. This is a basic misunderstanding. Little can be done about the problem as long as it is seen purely in biological terms. Penal administrators (and all who are interested in prisons) must be made to understand that most prison homosexuality is not a function of sexual deprivation itself. It is, rather, an expression of anger and aggression caused by the frustrations and indignities rooted in the nature of prison life as it exists today. Our prison inmates are not allowed to function as men who have rights and privileges, and it is the loss of "manhood" in the broadest sense that motivates prison homosexuality—not simply the absence of heterosexual intercourse.

As the Parchman inmates indicated, physical satisfaction is not the most important aspect of conjugal visits. The most important element is emotional satisfaction—its influence on his self esteem and emotional needs keeps a man who has conjugal visits from resorting to homosexuality. The visits allow him to retain a strong identification with his wife and children through personal interaction with them. And since he has this right, he is able to keep the self-image of a man who is still important to others. He also knows that the penitentiary officials think of him as a man since they give him the privilege.

It is on this level—the level of emotional values—that conjugal visiting must be understood. As long as prison administrators see conjugal visits as "legalized prostitution" and only a release from sexual tensions, they will never accept the practice. Such a dismissal of conjugal visiting in regard to sexual problems in prison is naive and reveals the lack of a mature approach to corrections in general.

Many object to the Mississippi system of conjugal visiting because it was unplanned and developed informally. Although prison administrators hesitate to follow a system which developed in this manner, it should be given consideration for this very reason. Rather than being the product of one man's thinking and planning, and thereby limited, it shows a naturalness not found in other systems. The developments which have occurred in conjugal visiting at Parchman are those which *work* and meet the needs of the inmates. It is not likely that any other prison can "transplant" the Mississippi system in its entirety, of course.

Nevertheless, all penal administrators should study it and use whatever aspects of the system are appropriate.

The fact that conjugal visiting developed in Mississippi has been a handicap to its acceptance in other prisons. Even though Parchman has changed, penologists still do not regard it as a system to follow. California's new program in conjugal visiting at Tehachapi, therefore, is very important. It provides a precedent of conjugal visiting in a prison system without the stigma of a bad reputation. Hopefully, other prisons in the United States will now be more willing to develop conjugal visiting programs. Mississippi's program, however, is much more extensive than California's and it should be studied carefully when new programs are planned. California's system has been developed thus far only for men who are ready for release. While a pre-release system of conjugal visiting is important, it does not go far enough to have a basic influence on the nature of prison sexual problems. If a man is sentenced to prison for three years, he needs the conjugal visiting privilege throughout the entire sentence, not just in the last few weeks. In Mississippi, there is an example of a system of conjugal visiting in which a prisoner may take part from the beginning of his sentence. It deserves the attention of all who are interested in corrections.

Bibliography

Books

Aid to Dependent Children in Mississippi. Jackson: State Department of Public Welfare, 1963.

Alexander, W. B. *The Lash*. Privately Published, 1959. (Copy in the University of Mississippi Library.)

Argyris, C. *Human Relations in a Hospital*. New Haven: Labor and Management Center, 1955.

Barnes, Harry Elmer, and Negley K. Teeters. *New Horizons in Criminology*. Englewood Cliffs: Prentice-Hall, 1959.

Beck, P. G., and M. C. Foster. *Six Rural Problem Areas: Relief-Resources-Rehabilitation*. Federal Emergency Relief Administration Research Monograph I. Washington, 1935.

Belcher, John C., and Morton B. King. *Mississippi's People*. University, Miss.: Bureau of Public Administration, University of Mississippi, 1950.

Bierstedt, Robert. *The Social Order*. New York: McGraw-Hill, 1957.

Boeger, E. A., and E. A. Goldenweiser. *A Study of the Tenant Systems of Farming in the Yazoo-Mississippi Delta*. U. S. Department of Agriculture Bulletin 337. Washington, 1916.

Brannon, C. O. *Relation of Land Tenure to Plantation Organization*. U.S. Department of Agriculture Bulletin 1269. Washington, 1924.

Clemmer, Donald. *The Prison Community*. New York: Rinehart, 1958.

Cloward, Richard A., and others. *Theoretical Studies in Social Organization of the Prison.* New York: Social Science Research Council, 1960.

Cressey, Donald, ed. *The Prison.* New York: Holt, Rinehart and Winston, 1961.

Dollard, John. *Caste and Class in a Southern Town.* New Haven: Yale University Press, 1937.

Elliott, Mabel A. *Crime in Modern Society.* New York: Harper, 1952.

Fenton, Norman. *The Prisoner's Family.* Palo Alto: Pacific Books, 1959.

———, ed. *Handbook on the Inmate's Relationships with Persons Outside the Adult Correctional Institution.* American Prison Association, Committee on Classification and Casework, 1953.

Fishman, Joseph. *Sex in Prison.* New York: National Library Press, 1934.

Hoffsomer, Harold C. *Landlord-Tenant Relation and Relief in Alabama.* Washington: Federal Relief Administration, 1935.

Howard, John. *State of the Prisons in England and Wales.* Warrington, England: William Eyres, 1784.

Johnson, Norman; Leonard Savits; and Marvin E. Wolfgang. *The Sociology of Punishment and Correction.* New York: John Wiley, 1963.

Kolb, John H., and Edmund Des Brunner. *A Study of Rural Society.* Boston: Houghton-Mifflin, 1952.

Landis, Paul H. *Rural Life in Progress.* New York: McGraw-Hill, 1948.

Loomis, Charles P., and J. Allen Beegle. *Rural Sociology.* Englewood Cliffs: Prentice-Hall, 1957.

Mack, Raymond W. *Race, Class and Power.* New York: American Book, 1968.

Martin, John Barlow. *Break Down the Walls.* New York: Ballantine Books, 1954.

Masters, William H., and Virginia E. Johnson. *Human Sexual Response*. Boston: Little, Brown, 1966.

McKelvey, Blake. *American Prisons*. Chicago: University of Chicago Press, 1936.

Nelson, Victor. *Prison Days and Nights*. Boston: Little, Brown, 1932.

Ogburn, William P., and Meyer F. Nimkoff. *Sociology*. Boston: Houghton-Mifflin, 1958.

Patterson, Haywood, and Earl Conrad. *Scottsboro Boy*. Garden City, N.Y.: Doubleday, 1950.

Public Welfare in Mississippi. Jackson: State Department of Public Welfare, 1962.

Report on Sexual Assaults in the Philadelphia Prison System and Sheriff's Vans. Philadelphia: Philadelphia District Attorney's Office and Police Department, 1968.

Rubin, Morton. *Plantation County*. Chapel Hill: University of North Carolina Press, 1951.

Simpson, George. *Emile Durkheim on the Division of Labor in Society*. New York: Macmillan, 1933.

Smith, T. Lynn. *The Sociology of Rural Life*. New York: Harper, 1953.

Sorokin, P. A., and Carle C. Zimmerman. *Principles of Rural-Urban Sociology*. New York: Henry Holt, 1929.

Stouffer, Samuel, and others. *The American Soldier*. 2 vols. Princeton: Princeton University Press, 1949.

Sutherland, Robert L.; Julien L. Woodward; and Milton A. Maxwell. *Introductory Sociology*. New York: J. B. Lippincott, 1961.

Sykes, Gresham M. *The Society of Captives*. Princeton: Princeton University Press, 1958.

Tannebaum, Frank. *Crime and the Community*. New York: Ginn, 1938.

Tappan, Paul W. *Crime, Justice and Correction*. New York: McGraw-Hill, 1960.

Teeters, Negley K. *Penology From Panama to Cape Horn.* Philadelphia: University of Pennsylvania Press, 1946.

Thomlinson, Ralph. *Population Dynamics.* New York: Random House, 1965.

Vedder, Clyde B., and Patricia G. King. *Problems of Homosexuality in Corrections.* Springfield, Ill.: Charles C. Thomas Books, 1967.

Whyte, William F. *Human Relations in the Restaurant Industry.* New York: McGraw-Hill, 1948.

Public Documents

Biennial Report of the Superintendent and Other Officers of the Mississippi State Penitentiary, July 1, 1961 through June 30, 1963.

General Law of Mississippi, 1960. Chapter 284.

Mississippi House Journal, 1914. pp. 67-68.

Mississippi State Constitution. Article X.

Progress Report, 1964–1968. Mississippi State Penitentiary, Parchman, Miss.

U.S. Bureau of the Census. *U.S. Census of Population, 1960; General Population Characteristics, Mississippi.* Final Report PC (1) –26B. Washington, 1961.

Articles

Balough, Joseph K. "Conjugal Visiting in Prisons: A Sociological Perspective." *Federal Probation,* XXVIII (1964), 52–58.

"Black Annie." *Newsweek,* March 18, 1963.

"Black Palace." *Life,* April 3, 1950.

Caldwell, Ronald. "Group Dynamics in the Prison Community." *Journal of Criminal Law, Criminology and Police Science,* XLVIII (1956), 61–68.

Cavan, Ruth Shonle, and Eugene S. Zemans. "Marital Relationships of Prisoners in Twenty-Eight Countries." *Journal of Criminal Law, Criminology and Police Science,* XLIX (July–August, 1958), 133–39.

Duffy, Clinton T. "Prison Problem Nobody Talks About." *This Week Magazine,* October 21, 1962.

Foreman, Paul B., and Julien R. Tatum. "A Short History of Mississippi's Penal System." *Mississippi Law Journal,* X, no. 3 (1938), 249–60.

Fox, Vernon. "The Effect of Counseling on Adjustment in Prison." *Social Forces,* XXXII (March, 1954), 285–89.

Fraser, A. G. "Lay Visiting in America." *Proceedings, National Association for Prison Visitors.* England, 1951.

Galtung, Johan. "The Social Functions of a Prison." *Social Problems,* VI (1958), 127–40.

Goffman, Erving. "On the Characteristics of Total Institutions: The Inmate World." In *The Prison,* edited by Donald Cressey. New York: Holt, Rinehart and Winston, 1961.

Hopper, Columbus B. "The Conjugal Visit at the Mississippi State Penitentiary." *Journal of Criminal Law, Criminology and Police Science,* LIII (September, 1962), 340–44.

Jewell, Donald P. "Mexico's Tres Marias Penal Colony." *Journal of Criminal Law, Criminology and Police Science,* XLVIII (1958), 410–13.

Jones, J. H. "Penitentiary Reform in Mississippi." *Publications of the Mississippi Historical Society,* VI (1902), 475–86.

Karpman, Ben. "Sex Life in Prisons." *Journal of Criminal Law and Criminology,* XXXVIII (1948), 475–86.

Knight, C. "Family Prison: Parchman Penitentiary." *Cosmopolitan,* March, 1960.

Landermann, Peter. "Life as a Soviet Prisoner." *Saturday Evening Post,* January 15, 1966.

McCleery, Richard H. "The Governmental Process and Informal Social Control." In *The Prison,* edited by Donald Cressey. New York: Holt, Rinehart and Winston, 1961.

McCorkle, Lloyd W. "Social Structure in a Prison." *The Welfare Reporter,* VIII (1955), 6–11.

———, and Richard Korn. "Resocialization Within Walls." *The Annals,* CCXCIII (1954), 89–98.

Mitler, Ernest A. "Family Visits Inside a Prison." *Parade,* May 17, 1959.

Mouledous, Joseph C. "Organizational Goals and Structural Change: A Study of the Organization of a Prison Social System." *Social Forces,* XLI (March, 1963) 283–90.

Riemer, Hans. "Socialization in the Prison Community." *Proceedings of the American Prison Association.* 1937, pp. 151–55.

Schrag, Clarence. "Some Foundations for a Theory of Correction." In *The Prison,* edited by Donald Cressey. New York: Holt, Rinehart and Winston, 1961.

Sykes, Gresham. "Men, Merchants, and Toughs: A Study of Reactions to Imprisonment." *Social Problems,* IV (October, 1956), 130–38.

———, and Sheldon L. Messinger. "The Inmate Social Code And Its Functions." In *The Sociology of Punishment and Correction,* edited by Norman Johnson and others. New York: John Wiley, 1963, pp. 92–98.

Teeters, N. K. "Prison Visiting in the Penal Program." *Journal of Criminal Law and Criminology,* XXX (November–December, 1939), 87–91.

Verborgen, Von Luzian. "Freiheitsstrafvollug und Ehelicher Umgang." *Monatsschrift Fur Kriminologie Und Strafrechtareform,* XLVI (1963), 200–22.

"Wedlock in the Cellblock." *Time,* May 5, 1952.

Wheeler, Stanton. "Role Conflict in Correctional Communities." In *The Prison,* edited by Donald Cressey. New York: Holt, Rinehart and Winston, 1961.

———, "Socialization in Correctional Communities." *American Sociological Review,* XXVI (October, 1961), 48–57.
Zemans, Eugene S., and Ruth S. Cavan. "Marital Relationships of Prisoners." *Journal of Criminal Law, Criminology and Police Science,* XLIX (1958), 56–57.

Newspapers and Periodicals

Baton Rouge *State-Times.* January 5, February 2, 1968.
Memphis *Commercial Appeal.* March 3, October 1, 1968.
Time. September 22, 1967; and August 9, 1968.

Unpublished Material

Hutson, Marvin Lee. "Mississippi's State Penal System." Master's Thesis, University of Mississippi, 1939.
Macknak, D. G. Personal correspondence, February, 1969.
Shivers, Lydia Gordon. "A History of the Mississippi Penitentiary." Master's Thesis, University of Mississippi, 1930.

Index

Accommodation: definition of, 73; in development of conjugal visiting, 73, 74. *See also* Captive-captor relationship

Age of prisoners: relating to conjugal visiting, 62, 63. *See* chap. 5 *passim*

American Correctional Association, 13

American Prison Association, 3

Arkansas prison system, 20, 81

Attitudes of inmates. *See* Inmate code, chap. 5 *passim*

Auburn System, 17

Barbieri, Judge Alexander F., 12*n*

"Black Annie" (also called "Bull Hide"), 34, 35, 36, 37

Board of Commissioners, 25, 26

Book Binding. *See* Vocational training

Breazeale, C. E., 37

Brewer, Governor Earl, 20, 21

Budget of Parchman, 23. *See also* Salaries

"Cages," 38

California Correctional Institute, 5, 148

Camp size: in development of conjugal visiting, 75, 76; importance to conjugal visiting, 77, 78, 79, 137, 140

Camps at Parchman: description of, 41–47; inmate population by, 41; importance of small camps, 75–79, 137, 140. *See also* Camp size

Captive-captor relationship, 112, 140–141. *See also* Accommodation

Cell-block system: in first Mississippi State Prison, 17, 18; in Maximum Security at Parchman, 46; as bar to conjugal visiting, 144

Chapel for inmates, 46, 55

Chaplain at Parchman, 26, 28

Children of prisoners, 57, 60

Civil War: impact of on the Mississippi prison system, 18, 19

Clemmer, Donald, 111–12

Clothing of inmates: elimination of stripes, 31; current, 113–14

Code. *See* Inmate code

Commissary: described, 27; users of, 27

Common-law marriage: in Mexico, 7; problems caused by at Parchman, 96

Conjugal visiting
—at Parchman: development of 52–55; major factors in development of, 64, 137, 139, chap. 3 *passim;* current program, 49–50, 55–63; evaluation of, chap. 5 *passim;* attitudes of prisoners to, chap. 4 *passim*
—in foreign countries: those not allowing, 5, 6; countries having, 6–8; in Mexico, 6–7, 9–10; in Soviet Union, 6; in Sweden, 7, 8
—future possibilities of, chap. 6 *passim*
—in California. *See* California Correctional Institute
Cook, Thomas D., 48, 144
Crops: revenues derived from, 23; acreage in cotton, 23; harvesting of, 24, 25; types of grown at camps, 41–47

Davies, Alan, 12n
Diagnostic Center at Parchman, 31
Diet: of inmates, 39, 40
Discipline of prisoners, 32–37
Dogs (Bloodhounds), 43, 58
"Drivers": assistant sergeants, 35, 39
Duffy, Clinton, 12, 13
Durkheim, Emile, 68n

"East Prison," 18
Economics: emphasized at Parchman, 20; importance in development of conjugal visiting, 74, 75, 135–37
Educational levels: of prisoners responding to questionnaire, 125

Educational program at Parchman, 31, 32
Elections: penitentiary as an issue in, 20
Escapes from Parchman, 57, 58

"Fags": explanation of, 85, 86
Family visiting at Parchman, 50, 56, 61, 71, 101, 105
First Offenders' Camp, 40, 41, 46
Friendships: among prisoners, chap. 5 *passim*
Furloughs: countries allowing only, 6; countries allowing conjugal visiting and, 6, 7, 8, 9; in Mississippi, 51; in Louisiana, 51; as opposed to conjugal visits, 145

"Gal boys," 94
Grades of inmates at Parchman, 113, 114
Guards: trusties used as, 38; civilian, 40; attitudes of toward conjugal visits, 89–98
"Gunline," 58
"Gunman." *See* Grades of inmates

Half-trusties at Parchman, 114
Harpole, William, 15
"Hog," 114, 116
Holiday Suspension Program, 51
Homosexuality: extent of in American prisons, 85; homosexual roles in prisons, 84–86; in Philadelphia Prison System, 86, 87; at Parchman, 90–95; reasons for, 146; effects of conjugal visiting on, 84–147 *passim*
Hospital at Parchman: description of, 45, 46

Howard, John, 110
Hypotheses tested, 111, 117, 118

Informality in conjugal visits, 52, 56, 58
Inmate code: tenets of, 115-17; hypotheses relating to, chap. 5 *passim;* in relation to conjugal visits, 137-39

Jackson, Miss., 17, 18, 19, 46
"Jockers," 86, 94

"Kid," 94

Lease system in Mississippi, 19
Leaves. *See* Furloughs
"Legs." *See* Half-trusties
Letters of inmates: censored, 89
Library at Parchman, 30
Louisiana penal system, 20, 51, 81
Loyalty among inmates, 117, 122, 123, 136. *See also* Friendships

Macknak, D. G., 12
Maria Madre. *See* Tres Maria Penal Colony
Marriage license: check for, 56, 63
Maximum Security at Parchman: used as punishment, 33; description of, 46
Methodology: research, 15, 16, 111, 117-20
Mississippi State Penitentiary (Parchman): acreage in, 17; history of, 17-22; description of, 23-24; salaries of employees, 28-30; changes occurring in, 47-48; development of conju-

gal visiting at, 64-83; in relation to other prisons, 137-148; mentioned, *passim. See also* Organization of the penitentiary

Newspaper of inmates: "Inside World," 32, 43
Night watchman, 39

Organization of the penitentiary: physical, 23, 24, 25; by camp function, 40; as a factor in development of conjugal visiting, 64, 137, 139

Parchman. *See* Mississippi State Penitentiary
Penal Colonies: countries having, 9; Tres Marias Penal Colony, 9-11
Philadelphia, Pa., 12
Physical examination of inmates, 46
Plantation system: importance of in conjugal visiting, 71-74, 137; mentioned, 17, 19, 23
Political appointments at Parchman, 20, 25
Prisonization: definition of, 111; determinants of, 111, 112; prison structure as a factor in, 112; at Parchman, 112-17, 110-36 *passim*
Profits: from penitentiary products, 23
Psychological testing of inmates, 31
Punishment: of prisoners, 32, 33; corporal, 34-36. *See also* Discipline
"Punk," 85, 86, 87, 94
Race. *See* Segregation of races

Recreation program: described, 32; proposed recreation center, 47.

"Red Houses," 40, 54, 55, 58–60, 62

Rifles used in guarding, 39, 40

"Right guy," 116

Riot: in Mexico, 7; at Parchman, 36

"Risky," 114. See also Grades of inmates

Rochester, Robert, 51n

Ross, Tom, 36

Salaries of employees, 28–30

Saskatchewan Correctional Centre, 12

Segregation of races: by camp, 37, 65; as factor in conjugal visiting development, 79, 80, 139; in data analysis, 120 123, 125, 126, 128, 130–32

Sergeants at Parchman: responsibility of, 24; attitude of, 59, 82; background of, 69; personal relationships with inmates, 77, 78; evaluation of conjugal visits, 90–97

Sexual adjustment in prison, 88, 89, 95

Sharp, E. Preston, 13

"Shooters," 39

Sing Sing, 24

Single men: attitude of, 98–101

"Sissies," 91, 92, 94

Smith, T. Lynn, 66

Southern Regional Council: and evaluation of Parchman, 23

Sports. See Recreation

Sunflower County, Miss., 17, 20

Superintendent: appointment of, 25; qualifications of, 25; duties of, 26, 27; mentioned, 37, 48, 144

Tres Marias Penal Colony, 9, 10

Trusties: used as guards, 38: other trusties, 39

Venereal disease: examination for, 46; and conjugal visiting, 97

Verborgen, Von Luzian, 5, 11

Visiting day at Parchman, 49–60 passim. See also Family visiting; Visiting privileges

Visiting privileges elsewhere: in U.S., 4, 148; in foreign countries, 5–12

Vocational training at Parchman: book binding, 30; trade schools, 30; bands, 32

Wardens' attitudes toward conjugal visiting, 13

Whipping of inmates. See "Black Annie"

"Wolves," 85, 94

Women: prisoners, 10, 60; Women's Camp, 40, 41, 45